WHAT IF GOD SENDS REVIVAL?

Kevin Kutcel's passion for revival has captured his attention and focus for years. Now, through this book, we get to benefit from his deep burden for revival. Above all, this book is a call for the church to truly pray for a revival in our time. May the Lord, indeed, bring revival.

**—David Lane,
Superintendent, Central District CMA,
Wadsworth, OH**

Kevin Kutcel has allowed his significant experience as a Pastor, Missionary, and avid reader to fill the pages of this helpful and inspiring work. As he breaks down common myths surrounding revival, the reader will find themselves longing for the Lord to bring a fresh revival to our dark world. Praise the Lord, if he can raise the dead, there is no doubt that He can revive our lives, our families, our churches, our country, and our world.

**—Shawn Brennan,
Pastor, Hope Church,
Brunswick, OH**

What If God Sends Revival? will ignite the desire for revival in your heart. Revival is the result of the prayers of God's people and this book will bring conviction why the church must pray for the next revival. Kevin Kutcel's passion for a genuine moving of God's Spirit upon our church is written on every page. I have been personally blessed by the ministry of Real Revival and Kevin's passion for God to send revival. I am confident that all who read this book will be blessed and convicted to pray for revival.

**—Dayle Keefer, Retired Pastor,
Fluvanna Community Church,
Jamestown, NY**

As President of Anchor of Hope, endorsing *What If God Sends Revival?* is rooted in my belief in the power of prayer to transform lives and communities. The message of praying for revival is urgently needed—our churches and world are facing crisis, spiritual apathy, and division, and only a move of God's Spirit can bring true healing and change. This book offers hope, scriptural direction, and practical encouragement for individuals and congregations longing to see God renew His people from the inside out. *What If God Sends Revival?* inspires and equips believers to pursue a deeper relationship with God, to pray expectantly, and to commit themselves to unity, repentance, and service. I wholeheartedly endorse this book, believing it can ignite a renewed passion for prayer and revival in churches and communities everywhere.

**—Ann-Marie Potemski,
Founder and President, Anchor of Hope Inc.,
Brunswick, OH**

WHAT IF GOD SENDS REVIVAL?

GOD'S PLAN TO TRANSFORM YOUR CHURCH, COMMUNITY, AND COUNTRY

KEVIN KUTCEL

What If God Sends Revival?

Copyright © 2025 Kevin Kutcel

All rights reserved. No portion of this book may be reproduced, stored in a retrieval system, or transmitted in any form or by any means—for example, electronic, mechanical, photocopy, recording, scanning, or other—except for brief questions in critical reviews or articles, without the prior written permission of the publisher.

Published by Free Agent Press

ISBN-13: 978-1-946730-40-4 (Hardcover)
ISBN-13: 978-1-946730-41-1 (Softcover)
ISBN-13: 978-1-946730-42-8 (E-book)

Edited by Amber Derr, TheEditDerr.com
Book design by James Woosley, FreeAgentPress.com

Published by Free Agent Press
FreeAgentPress.com
Satsuma, Alabama 36572
VID: 20251120

CONTENTS

Foreword xi
Author's Note.. xvii
Introduction 1
1 – What is Revival?.. 7
2 – Revival is Transformation.. 17
3 – Revival is the Movement of the Holy Spirit....... 31
4 – Prayer Ignites Revival 43
5 – Why Corporate Prayer? 59
6 – Revival Brings Change to the Church.................. 71
7 – What Makes a Revival Great?................................. 85
8 – Revival Will Change a Nation 95
9 – What If...Revival?.. 111
Conclusion 123
Letter to Pastors...127
Endnotes 133

FOREWORD

I **AM PROUD TO ADMIT** I am part of the Sunday School felt board generation. I have firsthand experience with being mesmerized watching those 2-D characters move across the board. As a little boy, after the Sunday school hour was over, I'd pick my own dream team of famous Bible felt heroes and take on the kingdom of darkness. Of course, I was right there in the middle of it all, being used by God to bring His kingdom, right next to Peter and Paul and Elijah and Joshua and David, and of course, Jesus. Jesus and I were undefeated in every adventure. As a child, I was raised and trained by my parents and my church family to have faith in being used by God. I was raised to believe this would happen to me.

In high school and into college, I was still dreaming. I started devouring books about the famous missionaries, the Great Awakening, and other revivals. I read all the biographies I could about those men and women so powerfully used by God, but I ran into several problems. First, as a child it seemed that we never really saw any stories with power and transformation of Biblical proportions. From grade school through college, I met more people trying to explain why this didn't happen anymore. Clearly, they needed to get themselves a felt board.

Another problem I had was that as I left high school and went to Moody Bible Institute for college, it became very apparent that I was just average. It was a letdown when President Joe Stowell, one of my heroes, didn't pick me out of the crowd; actually, no one picked me out of the crowd. What was more shocking was that after finishing my time at Moody, I sensed God calling me to be a pastor. I was stunned that God would pick me. I joined a long list of men and women on the felt board who have said to God, "Who, me? I'm just a dude like Gideon, trying not to get killed while making a good loaf of whole wheat bread. Who am I?"

But as I went into ministry, I realized I had yet another problem and it's still a big issue to this day. I wonder if you have the same problem that I have? Although I am still not a "Big Deal," I'm still a sucker for the dream that I could be part of another Great Revival. I'm still captivated by that felt board story of Jonah going to Ninevah and seeing a whole nation turn to God, and he was such a grump. I'm ruined. God has ruined me because I know it can happen again. I know it. Every story of the Bible tells me that even at 54 years old, there's still a chance. Do you feel it? Deep in your spirit? Created for more? Called for more?

I met Kevin about 8–10 years into my ministry. I knew I liked Kevin because he was crazy. Not in terms of being medically "admissible" but in terms of being captivated by this call of living by faith and praying for a movement of God as great as the Great Awakening. Look at his resume: Missionary to Poland? Church Planting? As a friend of Kevin, let me just tell you he is dangerous because he doesn't care much about what this world thinks in terms of success and fame. Church planters are nutters, to use British vernacular. But he wasn't crazy for crazy's sake. He and his wife, Katie, are a couple of deep faith, scholars of the Word, students of history, and ruined by the Word of God. They are believers for the impossible because God is still that same God we read about in the Bible and in world history. Deep faith runs in their home and marriage.

I have prayed with Kevin. We have been on our knees together, and I can tell you that he is a man who has lived for this and yearned for this. We have dreamed and been on our knees before

God, calling out to Him for Revival. Kevin lives this out. I've been there in times of prayer when his heart breaks for the lost. When he calls out yet again for God to move. I have seen the discipline and his endurance over time that outlasts the emotion or passion. I've been there to celebrate his firsthand accounts of miracles and breakthroughs—the stories of the gates of hell being ripped apart by the power of God. He has done the soul work that is required for a movement of God. He looks at his heart in deep and profound ways so that God can bless him. Kevin is by no means perfect, but neither were any of the other people up on the felt board except Jesus.

About eight years ago, I invited Kevin to preach a message on Revival at the church where I served for nineteen years. That message, which is part of this book, became one of the most listened to messages at that church over all the years I was the senior pastor. Yes, God has a sense of humor, but I told Him it was only mildly funny. I felt like D.L. Moody must have when he was out of town and got a telegram telling him to get home because a revival was breaking out in his church. God used Kevin to spark a hunger for prayer and faith for God to move. He came and preached on Revival two more times, and it translated into deeper and deeper expectation. God used Kevin to create this desire for a supernatural movement of God, dare we say, "A Revival."

So, here's the brass tacks: put your seat belt on. Kevin is going to take you through inspiring stories of some of the greatest revivals the Church has seen. You're going to find yourself putting this book down in the middle of chapters and getting on your knees, inspired to pray and call out for God to move in your church or your family or your city. Kevin brings fresh insights into why revivals happen and how they get started, and how to sustain them. As a pastor, he knows the uphill battle it is to lead a church towards Revival. He breaks it down to very practical steps on how to lead this in your own church. Honestly, it's dangerous to read this because you will find yourself, just like I did, doing it with the Holy Spirit's nudging and prompting. You're going to face a question: "If that's what it takes, I can totally do that, but do I want to do it?"

Hopefully, at the end of this book you'll find yourself ruined in the best sense of the word. Ruined for a new movement of God, drawn into a fresh season of a faith awakened at what God longs to do through you. Wondering aloud, "What if…Revival?"

–Scott Brooks,
Pastor, Renewal Church, Sarasota, FL

AUTHOR'S NOTE

THE PROCESS OF COMPLETING this book has been an adventure. I initially started writing this book in the fall of 2019 while I still owned a consulting company that specialized in registering disinfectants with the EPA and the Lord told me that it was not the right time. I was perplexed by this as I was really motivated, but had no clue that in a few months the entire nation would be engulfed in a pandemic and my business would explode as many companies sought to register disinfectants with the EPA. I share this because I feel that the timing for this book is much better now than before the pandemic. Back then very few people spoke of revival and when the word was mentioned, there was a certain degree of skepticism. After the pandemic, the term revival has become commonplace and is being used in the vernacular much more frequently.

Therefore, I believe the timing of this book is more appropriate because though revival is mentioned much more often, the meaning of that term is not consistent and can be misunderstood. This book seeks to clearly define the term and to explain from historical events exactly what that term means. Revival is not a new term, but has recently re-emerged. Therefore, it is important to appreciate what revival meant in the past and why it is something we should seek for our future.

I am grateful to the many people who supported, prayed for, and encouraged me along the way. I deeply appreciate my wife, Katie, who greatly encouraged me in the process. To those who read early drafts and offered insightful feedback, your encouragement gave me confidence to keep refining the message. Finally, I am thankful for my friends, fellow pastors, and prayer partners who share my passion for revival and helped shape this book.

Finally, I thank the Lord for His patience and faithfulness in my life. The same God who poured out His Spirit in generations past continues to call His people to pray and believe for revival today. It is my prayer that this book inspires many to do just that, to seek Him with perseverance and faith until He moves again.

INTRODUCTION

WHY SHOULD WE SEEK another revival for our country? There are many misunderstandings regarding our history, but the Great Awakenings had a profound impact on our culture and dramatically shifted the values of our country. There have been four Great Awakenings, and without these revivals, we would be a different country today. Our history is not a straight line in which the founding was the pinnacle of virtue that slowly decayed into godless immorality. The embracing of Christianity by our country has multiple high and low points throughout our history. The peak is the early 20th century after the last great revival swept through our country, but like any roller coaster, the ride is full of ups and downs along the way.

I have always loved history, and about twenty years ago, I became familiar with the Great Awakenings. Though I knew about the revivals as a historical event and some of the main characters, I had no idea how dramatic their impact was upon our country. Like most people, I would have said that our country was founded as a "Christian nation," but I learned that the values we often associate with this statement were not due to the Second Continental Congress or the Constitutional Convention, but the Second Great Awakening that turned the country upside down. This Awakening not only spread the gospel like an uncontrollable wildfire but changed the entire landscape of the United States. It scorched the country with the power of the Holy Spirit and shifted the majority of opinion from having a secular viewpoint to a Christian worldview. Within ten years, the country went from being godless to desiring that the gospel of Jesus Christ be known around the world.

When I started preaching about these revivals and the impact they had on our country, people were amazed, and I realized how few were aware of this history. As Christians, we want all people to be saved, and we want the church to have an impact on our culture so that being a Christian is not only accepted, but widespread and influential, changing the worldview of the culture. This is exactly what the revivals accomplished.

My main motivation in writing this book is not to provide a history lesson but to motivate the church to pray. The only reason the past revivals occurred is that the Church united together as one and prayed with perseverance for revival. As far as I am aware, no revival has ever occurred without persevering prayer beforehand. I believe this is the real solution for our church, community, and country. Yes, we must be making disciples as Jesus told us in the Great Commission, but if we pray for revival, God will till the soil so disciple-making will be much more productive.

This is not a history book but a book that hopefully will give you an understanding of what God has done and will do if you pray for a pouring out of His Holy Spirit upon the Church. It is a book that will hopefully motivate your church to pray expectantly for another revival. That is the real solution for the fundamental issues we face today as the Church. In this book, I first define what revival is, since there are many misunderstandings regarding that word. I then describe how revival is initiated both from the scriptures and history and why corporate prayer is essential for a great revival to occur. The book then explains how revival will change your church, your community, and your country. Finally, I explain what is unique about a Great Awakening compared to many other revivals that occur at a local level.

My goal is this book will motivate a group of people in your church to start praying for the next revival. If hundreds of churches across denominational lines could begin praying for revival, I believe that this would have a dramatic impact upon our country. The Holy Spirit would awaken the masses to the gospel of Jesus Christ, many would be saved, and the trajectory of our country would be changed. History shows that when the Holy Spirit moves in power upon the country, change is inevitable.

The Great Awakenings in our past did not just happen. They occurred because the preceding generations cared enough about the declining condition of the Church and the country that they made corporate prayer for revival a priority and even signed covenants that they would pray until God brought revival, or they died. They were faithful in persistently praying for several years with no results being evident until suddenly the Holy Spirit swept upon the country with great power. Those generations earnestly believed what probably seemed impossible. It is our turn now, and we have been handed the baton. Each generation makes their own choices regarding what they will do. History is not inevitable or predetermined but a collection of choices made by people just like us. Yes, God is sovereign, but He responds to our faithfulness, and His Spirit will only come when we exhibit persevering faith that He can and will pour out His Spirit.

As a pastor, I am also motivated to speak about these great revivals and how they impacted the country. The stories are fascinating and almost unbelievable, except the firsthand historical accounts verify their authenticity. I would welcome the opportunity to share these stories in your church. Again, this book provides glimpses of each revival to illustrate the main point of the chapter, but it does not provide the complete story of each Great Awakening. I would love a chance to do that by engaging your congregation on how each Awakening dramatically changed our country. Please go to www.realrevival.com to learn how you can participate in this network of churches praying and how you can contact me.

CHAPTER 1

WHAT IS REVIVAL?

Revival is the visitation of God which brings to life Christians who have been sleeping and restores a deep sense of God's near presence and holiness.

—J.I. Packer

I WAS SITTING IN A prayer meeting with a group of pastors, and one said, "There is a revival occurring with our young people. I don't like to use that word, but I cannot think of a better word to describe what is occurring. God is really doing something, and I am excited about it." The pastor then described how their entire youth group was turning to Christ and the excitement they had about sharing their faith. This is the heart of what a revival is as people come to Christ. But why was he hesitant to describe this circumstance as a revival? Why do many people, including pastors, have a negative connotation with the term "revival" and avoid using it when the Holy Spirit is obviously at work?

"Revival" brings all kinds of images to people when they hear this word. Some people think of mass hysteria with Christians doing crazy things such as barking or dancing or anything else you can imagine. Others think of the tent being put up in front of the church with a huge sign along the highway saying "Tent Revival" as if a sign can create a revival.

> **"Revival" means that you are bringing a person back to life.**

"Revival" means that you are bringing a person back to life. We have no problem using the term in the medical community. "He stopped breathing, but the nurse was able to revive him." This does not create mass hysteria. We don't have a picture of the nurse jumping up and down on his chest, chanting incantations in the hope he will come back to life. No, we understand that the patient was not breathing and near death, and the nurse did his or her job, and the patient is now alive.

Revival means the same in the church as it does in the hospital. The person was dead and is now alive. But in the church, it means that the person was spiritually dead. The person has been revived. This is wonderful news! The Bible tells us that we were all dead in our sins but made alive by the Spirit. Every person who repents and accepts Christ has been revived!

First, we often think of "revival" only as a major event or mass movement of people. Revival is not describing an event but describing the before and after condition of a person, whether it is one or millions of people. If one person is saved or an entire stadium, revival has occurred for each of those people, regardless of the circumstances of the event. In my life, I was revived along with about a dozen other people after watching *The Cross and the Switchblade* at a Baptist Church. The event was not advertised as a revival, but the changes in my life were. Likewise, a revival does not depend upon specific characteristics other than people who were dead are now coming to life. Calling an event a "revival" without people's lives being transformed is like a church having a bake sale with nothing on the tables to sell. It may build expectations, but it is empty and meaningless.

One person being revived is exciting, but hundreds is a party! In Acts 2:41, it says that about three thousand were revived that day. That is a major celebration. Whether it is one person or three thousand, it is a revival for each person being saved. Again, revival is the change of the spiritual condition of the person, not the description of an event. Unfortunately, people often think of revival as an event involving a mass movement of people and dismiss the spiritual significance of the term for each person who has been saved.

Second, we can characterize a revival as only having certain characteristics, such as wild hysteria, because every revival is vastly different. In fact, many of our revivals have focused on prayer and were very organized with no sensationalism associated with them. The "Prayer Revival" of 1857 is characteristic of this. This revival started with daily prayer and its entire focus was organized prayer as it swept through the country.

Originally a shoe salesman with little formal education, Dwight L. Moody became one of the most influential evangelists during the "Prayer Revival" of 1857. His revivals were not characterized by hysteria or wild antics, but rather by a genuine transformation through the power of the gospel. Moody's meetings, often held in large venues like the Hippodrome in New York City, drew thousands of people who were eager to hear his simple, yet profound, messages of faith and redemption. Moody's approach to revival was methodical and deeply personal. He focused on the individual spiritual awakening rather than the spectacle of a mass movement. This personal touch resonated with people across social and economic lines, leading to significant spiritual revivals in the communities he visited. Moody's revivals were marked by a profound sense of peace and joy, as individuals who once felt spiritually dead found new life and purpose.

If you attend an NFL football game, you would assume that the atmosphere will be crowded and loud, with lots of beer and celebrations. But is the actual game the rowdy crowd or the players on the field? Of course, it is the players who play the game. In 2016, I went to a Cleveland Browns football game. This was the season that the Browns were 1-15. I did not see their only win. By the fourth quarter, we were the only ones sitting in our section. As a matter of fact, I don't believe there were more than 500 people in the entire stadium, which has over 50,000 seats. Was I still attending a football game? Yes, but there was no celebration and no crowd. Okay, maybe there were some people drinking beer, but not as much as the franchise was hoping for. Though we still attended a football game, it was uncharacteristic of the vast majority of NFL games played each Sunday. In the same way, revival is not dependent on the number of people present or how people are responding, but it is totally dependent on people being transformed by the Holy Spirit. Transformation is the "real game" of revival, not the other activities that may accompany it.

> **Revival is the rebirth of the soul of an individual regardless of the setting (2 Cor. 5:17).**

Revival must be appreciated for what it is and not be characterized for what it is not. Revival is the rebirth of the soul of an individual regardless of the setting (2 Cor. 5:17). By associating it with the environment, revival can be viewed as something to be avoided. Whether the revival involves one person or millions, there is great reason to celebrate. By avoiding the term, we are indirectly moving away from something I believe is at the heart of God, which is to revive people from death to life.

Revival is a wonderful event for each individual, whether the person is by himself or herself in a quiet room or in a stadium filled with thousands of people. Of course, it is more exciting to see hundreds and even thousands of people converted from death to life, so we should all celebrate such events. In the history of revivals, there are many different examples of a few to millions of people being converted. Every event is worthy of celebration regardless of the number or the circumstances of the event. Revival has occurred because people who were dead are now alive.

So let's embrace the term "revival" and understand its significance for the Church, our communities, and our country. By avoiding the term, we are diminishing what God has done in our history and what He can do in our future. If God can save one person in a revival, then He surely can save many. This is not to ignore the importance of every soul that is saved, but it is to challenge the notion that God only saves one person at a time. In the Bible, there are many instances of entire households being saved, and in the early church, over 3000 were added to their number after Peter's sermon (Acts 2:14–41). In a great revival, this is the norm rather than the peculiar. Regardless of the number, God receives the glory, but He desires for all to be saved which His Spirit can do in great abundance and power.

By concluding that revivals are only manufactured demonstrations of man-made hysteria, we can limit what God wants to do. We should avoid making these conclusions. Of course, there are limited instances where excesses occurred that raised questions about the genuineness of the revival. But the vast majority of revivals resulted in many people being saved, joining the Church, and changing society. The Great Revivals, which will be discussed later, resulted in millions of people being saved in a very short period of time changing the course of history for our country. God is not limited by what He can do through the power of the Holy Spirit when the Spirit is poured out upon a nation, but we can limit what God wants to do through unbelief or misconceptions without knowing the truth of what He has done. The purpose of this book is to encourage Christians to understand what revival is, what God has done, and to desire that He can and will do the same again if we believe and pray for it.

> **The purpose of this book is to encourage Christians to understand what revival is, what God has done, and to desire that He can and will do the same again if we believe and pray for it.**

Revivals are always occurring in various parts of the world at different times. However, every revival is the direct result of people believing God and praying for revival long before it occurs. It means that the Church must unite together and be motivated to pray for revival. Thus, the responsibility for revival happening rests with the Church. Usually, this occurs when the Church is despairing and believes that if God does not pour out His Spirit, there is little hope.

Most often in our history, though, this is not the case. The Church can easily exist without being desperate. As long as the bills are being paid and people are relatively content, why should we be desperate? Afterall, does it affect the Church if the vast majority of people in our community are not saved? That fact rarely brings desperation. Desperation is only felt when the church is losing members and cannot pay its bills, or when the Church is under pressure from society that it will no longer exist or be viable. Though this seems dramatic, this is the desperation that led churches to join together and pray corporately for the pouring out of His Spirit.

In the beginning of our nation, the Church was completely desperate because church attendance was at its lowest in our history and many were turning away from Christianity as having the answers for life. The feeling in the 1780s was if God did show up in a miraculous way, the doors of Christianity would be closed. This was even proclaimed boldly by the patriot, Thomas Paine. That is real desperation! This will be discussed in more detail in chapter 6.

Likewise, in the upper room in Acts 1, were the apostles feeling desperate? Yes, they had seen the resurrected Jesus and His ascension, but what do they do now? Jesus told them to wait and not leave Jerusalem, but wait for what? Jesus always had the answers and a great game plan, but He was gone. Yes, I believe there was a feeling of desperation when they prayed in the upper room. They had no real game plan and had real enemies in Jerusalem who were seeking to snuff out anyone who said they believed Jesus was the Messiah. Again, this is desperation. It is difficult to be motivated to pray when everything is going well and you are not facing a crisis in your life.

God wants to pour out His Spirit and bring revival to His church that would pour into our communities. God wants all people to be saved. God knows that we will pray when we are desperate and so He often allows situations to occur that are wake up calls for our churches. Yes, it would be much easier if God just poured out His Spirit without praying, but then we would think we somehow manufactured the revival with a great program and God would not be glorified. It is the complete dependency upon God that enables His Spirit to respond and we then understand that only God could do what just occurred. The question is how desperate the Church must become before we unite as one praying earnestly that His Spirit will be poured out upon our churches?

This is the desperation that conceives the mighty prayers of the saints to unleash the power of the Holy Spirit on His Church. Revival is a wonderful event and we should seek it with all our hearts and not be afraid of it, whether it is for one person or an entire nation. Revival is a miracle that is result of the Church praying and believing that God will be glorified. A Great Revival has not occurred for over a hundred years in our nation. Though there have been many small revivals, including ones that impacted large groups of people, we have not experienced a Great revival that swept the entire nation since the Welsh revival that occurred in the USA in 1904–1905. By understanding the power of revival and God's heart, may we embrace revival and believe that God wants to do in our generation what he has done for previous generations.

So, let's not fear the term "Revival" as we discuss what God is doing in our midst. If people are being saved, then God has brought revival. Let's pray for more revival and a mighty pouring out of His Spirit upon our people and His Church. Revival is good. Let's praise the Lord for each person who has been revived. If someone acts as if the term should be avoided in the Church, please remind them that only God can bring revival to His Church. The reason the pastor at the beginning of this chapter could not think of a better word to use is because there is no better word. Revival rocks and must be celebrated!

CHAPTER 2

REVIVAL IS TRANSFORMATION

> If your Christian conversion did not reverse the direction of your life, if it did not transform it then you are not converted at all. You are simply a victim of the "accept Jesus" heresy!
>
> —A.W. Tozer

VERY FEW PEOPLE LIKE to attend funerals because it is a reminder of the mortality of our lives. The fact that we will not live forever is even more vivid when the casket is open and we can see the person who died. Though this custom is disappearing because we want to pretend that we will never die, it is a pointed reminder that we do die. But even if we see the person lying there, we can still pretend that there is another reality, which is what I experienced. The funeral had an open casket, and I stood in line.

As I approached the person lying in the casket, the woman standing next to me suddenly exclaimed, "Doesn't she look good? She looks so peaceful. I think she is asleep!" I looked at the woman to see if she was joking, but she was not. The woman was serious. Inside, I was laughing and crying as I thought to myself, "You are talking about a person who is dead and there is no life." But this woman felt better by pretending that the person in the casket was okay because the funeral director had succeeded in putting some makeup on her face. Pretending does not change the situation, though. The person is dead. She is not coming back to life. Putting makeup on a dead person may make them look better, but it does nothing to bring the person back to life.

> **We need transformation, not reformation. Reformation is only changing the outer form, but transformation is changing the heart.**

The same is true for our spiritual lives and the life in our churches. We can go through life pretending everything is okay, but if you are spiritually dead, there is no amount of makeup that will give you a new life. We need transformation, not reformation. Reformation is only changing the outer form, but transformation is changing the heart. Transformation is when the Holy Spirit transforms the soul of the person creating a new person in Jesus Christ. Reformation is when we try to educate a person or change their behavior hoping that it will also change their heart. Transformation is from the inside out and not vice versa, but reformation seems much more doable because transformation is humanly impossible. After all, it is easier to put makeup on the dead person than to bring them back to life. The person in the casket has no hope of living again, but a spiritually dead person has wonderful hope, but it can only occur through the power of the Holy Spirit through a new birth.

The story of Abraham, as recorded in Genesis, is an amazing story of obedience. Most of us could never consider doing everything he did in following God. He was faithful in believing God by moving his family to a new country and was even willing to sacrifice his son at an altar because God commanded him to do so. We cannot comprehend the sacrifice that he made in his heart as he took Isaac to the altar, looked into his eyes, and raised the knife with the intent to plunge that instrument in his hands deep into the heart of his beloved son and murder him. It was an act of extreme obedience that none of us could ever comprehend. Yet was the obedience of Abraham what transformed him to be a follower of God? Many would say "Yes." Abraham proved his love for God by his radical obedience, but this is not what transformed him.

In Romans 4, the Apostle Paul points out that Abraham did not reform himself by obedience but was transformed by faith.

Paul makes a clear argument that "Abraham believed God, and it was credited to him as righteousness." What does it mean that it was "credited" to him? Did Abraham earn it? Was it a credit added to his account? No, Paul is stating that the righteousness imputed to Abraham made him into a different person. In other words, Abraham did not reform himself into being a God follower, but God transformed Abraham by imputing righteousness into his life and making him into a different person. God transformed Abraham because Abraham believed God. There was no amount of obedience, even a willingness to kill his own son, which would have transformed Abraham, but only God could do it through His Spirit imputing righteousness into the life of Abraham. It was that transformation that then allowed Abraham to be obedient as a follower of God. This assertion by Paul in chapter four of Romans was shocking to his audience as he declared that the great Patriarch Abraham did not earn righteousness through obedience but was transformed by faith.

If Abraham could not earn salvation through obedience, why do we believe we can today? Of course, most Christians understand that salvation occurs through faith in Christ. But do we practice this in the Church? Do we believe that the only hope of being righteous is by faith in Christ? The easy answer is yes, but is that the honest answer? Will God condemn a "good" person who is very faithful in doing many awesome deeds in church but never recognizes that they are spiritually dead? The person can look very good. The makeup of good works can look really convincing to other churchgoers, but a person is either alive or dead. There is no third choice. Who are we to judge if a person is alive or dead? We cannot, but we also should not pretend that spiritual death is okay.

We must be clear that without God's imputed righteousness in our souls, we are dead. This means we need to recognize that we are spiritually dead, and no amount of Bible knowledge and good works will save us. There is no transformation without repentance and faith. No amount of good works can bring life to a dead soul.

> **There is no transformation without repentance and faith. No amount of good works can bring life to a dead soul.**

We need to understand that every conversion is a miracle, just like a newborn baby. Through genetics and DNA, we now understand how a baby is formed, yet we still all understand that new life is a miracle. Every baby that enters this world is a miracle from God with their own personality and abilities. In the same way, every Christian is a miracle from God. This is why Jesus told us that the only way to enter heaven was by being born again. This is not a cute metaphor from Jesus, but an actual truth. A newborn baby only comes into the world by the union of the sperm and egg. No matter how much someone may want a new baby, unless this occurs, it will not happen.

In the same way, a Christian only comes to new birth through the Holy Spirit coming into their life and forming a new union with their spirit or soul. This is a miracle. That is why Paul said to the Corinthians that every person in Christ is a new creation; the old is gone, and the new has come. Again, this is not a cute metaphor. Paul is saying that a Christian really has a new life because they have a new birth due to the Holy Spirit in their life. Only God can perform this miracle. The miracle occurs when we understand that we are spiritually dead and that we need a Savior who will give us a new life. I cannot make myself righteous through good works. In other words, we need a revived soul.

This is why revival is considered transformation. Revival is bringing life to someone who is dead. To be revived, you must first recognize that you are spiritually dead and you need a Savior. You are either alive in Christ or you are dead in your sins. At some point in time, you choose to believe, and through faith in Christ, you are reborn. It is an event, not a process. Just like a particular time, Abraham believed God, and it was "credited" to him as righteousness. Before that time, he was not righteous, and afterwards, he was righteous. I understand that there are many Christians who cannot point to a specific time or event when they were saved, yet their faith in Christ is genuine and obvious. However, I believe that there was still a specific time in their life when they understood that they were a sinner who could not save themselves and believed that Christ died on the cross for their sins and chose to believe that. Even if they do not recall the event, it still occurred. You cannot be partially saved or be saved over time. You are either dead or alive.

Revival requires a recognition of our spiritual condition that we are spiritually dead. This can be very difficult for a person who is genuinely good. This was the stumbling block for the Pharisees and also for many proud people in the church. Only the Holy Spirit can bring a person to the recognition of their genuine spiritual condition. As Christians, it is obvious and easy to understand that we need a Savior. Many people are blinded from this truth, though. They can have Bible knowledge without recognizing their need of a Savior in their life. Just like the woman in the casket; no amount of makeup will substitute for the reality that we are spiritually dead without Christ. We will never earn God's love by our work in the church. I believe that this recognition of our spiritual condition and the need for a revival is the work of the Holy Spirit opening our eyes to the truth of our condition: no more pretending but being confronted with the truth of God that we are dead. Only the Holy Spirit can do this work so that we see the truth.

When I was a church planter, our church was growing as we met Sunday mornings in a social hall. Though God had provided the social hall for a good price, it was not the most conducive environment for us to have worship services as the smell of stale cigarette smoke and alcohol often hung in the air from the parties the night before. We did our best to air out the place, but it was a distraction. As I prayed about the situation, I believed that God was challenging us to build a new building a block away. In working with a local real estate agent, they owned a piece of property and they would build the steel shell and we would frame it out on the inside and do all the interior construction. Then we would rent the building with an option to purchase it. The only problem was the church had no money for this project. Any reasonable person would say moving forward without at least a portion of the money in the bank would be preposterous. But I spent time in the presence of God and I was convinced that the Lord was saying to trust Him and He would provide.

As we were planning to proceed, a wealthy businessman in our congregation challenged me by saying that this was the craziest decision as the "Lord gave us common sense and we needed to use it." This man had attended Bible Study Fellowship for many years and knew the stories of the Bible very well. When he said, "common sense," something went off inside of me and I responded, "So it was common sense that led Noah to spend 100 years building an ark in the middle of the desert in preparation for a flood even though it had never rained before? Or maybe it was common sense that Abraham used when he moved his family to an unknown place and believed God would give him a son even though he and Sarah were in their 90s." He quickly got my point and proceeded to leave the Church. Through many miracles, God gave us the building. I don't know the spiritual condition of that person, but I have learned that faith does not come from Bible knowledge, only from the Holy Spirit as a person is transformed into a new life believing that God can and will do the impossible. This person had a solid grasp of scripture, but that was not enough for him to trust that God could do the impossible or at least what made little sense in his mind.

How can we judge if a person really has repented of their sins and sought revival of their souls? We cannot, and only God knows. However, we need to stress the spiritual reality that everyone is dead and that we all need a Savior. We also need to pray for the Holy Spirit to speak to each person to open their eyes to their spiritual condition. If a person cannot specify a specific time when they repented and accepted Christ, we should at least ask them if they understand that our relationship with the Lord is completely dependent upon our new life in Christ.

In addition, a person who is a new creation in Christ is a person of faith. This person has a genuine relationship with the Lord that allows them to trust the Lord in the midst of difficult decisions.

They understand that God is totally sovereign and trustworthy. A person reliant on good works will not have that relationship and will be more reliant on reason in their decision-making. Though God exists, and they can understand that God is mighty and powerful, they do not have that intimate relationship with God to trust Him in their daily decisions.

Isaac Backus was instrumental in the Second Great Awakening in organizing all the churches in New England to be praying for revival. He wrote a letter to all denominational leaders in 1794 calling for the churches to pray. Backus' own transformation occurred during the First Great Awakening in 1741. Jonathan Edwards came to his hometown of Norwich, Connecticut, and he was motivated "to go and hear the most powerful preaching that I could," and even though many people were greatly moved by the preaching of Edwards, it had little effect on Backus. At that moment, he felt he was okay as he attended church regularly, learned the catechism, participated in family prayers, and was expected to become a church member when he married. He did not find the need to repent as he heard Edwards preach, but admitted later that "the Lord was letting me see something of the plague of my heart and the foundation of corruption that was there, so I began to worry for some weeks."[1] Suddenly, on August 29, 1741, as he was mowing the field alone, he suddenly became aware of his need for a Savior.

> *"It appeared to clear to me that I had tried every way that possibly that I could for salvation and if I perished forever I could do no more—and the justice of God shined so clear before my eyes in condemning such a guilty rebel that I could*

say no more—but fell at his feet. I saw that I was in the hands and he had the right to do with me just as he pleased. As I lay like a dead, vile creature before him. And just in that critical moment, God, who caused the light to shine out of darkness-shined into my heart with such a discovery of that glorious righteousness which fully satisfied the law that I had broke, and of the infinite fullness that there is in Christ to satisfy the wants of such a helpless creature as I was…that my whole heart was attracted and drawn after God and swallowed up in admiration in view of his divine glories. And now my Burden that was so dreadful heavy before was gone: that tormenting fear that I had was taken away, and I felt a sweet peace and rejoicing in my soul."[2]

Isaac Backus had been transformed by the Holy Spirit. However, when he returned to his parish church, he no longer found any comfort from the preaching and no reinforcement from the congregation that included many unconverted people according to Backus. When he and others who had been transformed asked the minister to exclude from membership those who experientially did not know Christ, he refused and so they left the church and formed a "separate church" meeting in a private home.[3]

Billy Graham tells the story of a woman named Mary, who had been attending church every Sunday for thirty years, but found herself deeply moved at his crusade in New York City. Despite her regular attendance and participation in church activities, Mary realized that something was missing in her spiritual life. As she listened to Graham's message about repentance and salvation, she felt as though he was speaking directly to her soul. Mary had always been regarded as a devoted churchgoer by her friends and family, but the truth was that she had never truly understood the significance of trusting Christ as her Savior.

In that moment, she experienced a profound spiritual awakening, a realization that attending church, while valuable, was not a substitute for a personal relationship with God. She realized though religiously active, she was spiritually dead. She needed revival, a deep and personal commitment to her faith that went beyond external appearances. Just like the woman in the casket, Mary was spiritually dead and she recognized it. Inspired by the Holy Spirit, Mary stepped forward during the altar call, joining thousands of others who had come to the same realization. This decision marked a pivotal moment in her life, leading her to a deeper understanding of her faith and a renewed sense of purpose.[4]

As I stated earlier, we need transformation and not reformation. Repentance and salvation are works of God that occur through the work of the Holy Spirit, prompting our soul to repent and need a Savior. It is coming to the reality that the person in the casket is me, and though I have used a lot of makeup to look good to everyone around me, God looks at me and knows the truth. I need the miracle of a rebirth in my life.

> **Revival conjures up many images, but the heart of revival is transformation.**

Revival conjures up many images, but the heart of revival is transformation. Of course, the desire is for the transformation to occur in many people and not just one person. Our desire for revival is for God to work in the church bringing many to revival which will then spread to the community and beyond. But revival is an inner work of the soul of the person regardless of the form it may take. Revivals have come in many forms, but genuine revival always results in transformation. The issue is when the church focuses on replicating a certain form and then pretending it is a revival (as if a revival can be manufactured by reliving the forms of past revivals).

The truth is a revival can manifest in different ways. Some revivals have been very quiet such as the Great Prayer Revival of 1857. Other revivals were known for many manifestations of the Holy Spirit such as Azusa Street and the Kentucky Campfire Meetings. Regardless of the form, the genuineness of the revival is determined by transformation. Are the people repentant and fully surrendered to the Lord to do His work in their lives? That is revival.

So, we should not shy away from seeking revival because we associate the term with a certain expression that makes us fearful, but we must embrace revival because of what it means in the hearts of individuals when the Holy Spirit moves in power. We cannot manufacture revival, nor can we control the work of the Holy Spirit. A genuine revival will be determined by the fruit it produces in the lives of the individuals that it touches. It will bring transformation to the Church and to the surrounding areas. It cannot be controlled, but it can be quenched by a lack of continual prayer and belief.

If people are being transformed, we should rejoice that revival is occurring. Too often, when the Holy Spirit starts working, our response is to judge if what is occurring is genuine or not. If people are repenting of their sins and professing Christ as their Savior and Lord, that is not the work of the devil. Only the Holy Spirit can do this work in a person's life. We have a tendency to judge too quickly and sadly quench the work of the Holy Spirit. The proper response is to continue to seek the Lord and pray. As long as people are repenting and people are being saved, God is at work. People are being transformed into a new life versus putting make-up on a dead person to make them look better.

There are plenty of examples of people trying to manufacture a revival. Those efforts are short-lived and bear no fruit. The person in the coffin is not going to look or smell good for very long regardless of the amount of make-up or perfume being used. After a couple of days, it is time to close the lid and bury the coffin. The same with a revival that is man-made. However, if the person in the coffin comes to life and gets out of the coffin, please don't try to control the reaction in the audience. You will become a fool. People will be in shock and overwhelmed with joy. It will be reported for miles and be in every news outlet. Suddenly what is impossible has become possible.

Jesus proved this when he raised Lazarus from the dead in John 11. Everyone knew that Lazarus was dead because he had been in the tomb for four days. Jesus even delayed his journey to Bethany to be sure everyone understood that Lazarus had really died. Yes, Lazarus was really dead, but as Jesus proclaims in John 11:25, "I am the resurrection and the life. He who believes in me will live, even though he dies; and whoever lives and believes in me will never die. Do you believe this?" Then when they roll away the stone, Martha questions what Jesus is saying by proclaiming that

Lazarus is dead and there will be a bad odor. But Jesus tells her, "Did I not tell you that if you believed, you would see the glory of God?"

> **Likewise, during a revival, the Holy Spirit proves who He is by transforming people to real life and suddenly people cannot deny the reality of the power of God in their midst.**

When Lazarus comes out of the tomb, many put their faith in Jesus. Jesus did not put make-up on Lazarus and pretend that he was alive. Lazarus was alive! This was a great cause for celebration. And word spread quickly to Jerusalem where the Pharisees knew that they had a serious problem because the Messiah had proven who He was in Bethany. Likewise, during a revival, the Holy Spirit proves who He is by transforming people to real life and suddenly people cannot deny the reality of the power of God in their midst. Abraham believed God and was transformed by the Holy Spirit. Knowing God intellectually is not the same as transformation of the soul where you are willing to put your trust in a mighty God who can do the impossible.

CHAPTER 3

REVIVAL IS THE MOVEMENT OF THE HOLY SPIRIT

> What the Church needs today is not more machinery or better, not new organizations or more and novel methods, but men whom the Holy Ghost can use—men of prayer, men mighty in prayer. The Holy Ghost does not flow through methods, but through men. He does not come on machinery, but on men. He does not anoint plans, but men—men of prayer.
>
> —E.M. Bounds,
> *Power Through Prayer*

ONE TIME OUR CAR would not start, and we could not figure out why. The gas gauge said that there was a quarter tank, and the battery was clearly good, but the engine was not getting any gas. We made the assumption that the gas pump located in the gas tank was not working. So, we jacked up the car and proceeded to slowly remove the bolts that held the straps which kept the gas tank in place. It was slow, painful work as the bolts were rusted, but we slowly succeeded. Finally, we removed the straps and prepared ourselves to remove the gas tank. According to the gauge, there were about four gallons of gasoline left in the tank. But in removing the final strap, the tank dropped, and it was as light as a feather. The gas tank was bone dry! The problem was not the gas pump, but the fact that there was no gas in the tank. The gas gauge was broken. Once we put gas in the tank, the car started. We had just wasted several hours of our time removing a gas tank from the car when all we needed to do was put gas into the car! Should we laugh or cry? I think we did both.

Just as the car must have gas to run, revivals only occur through the work of the Holy Spirit. It is so simple, but we wrestle with this truth because God sends His Spirit as we pray and fast. We all wish there was another way around this because praying requires work, focus, and faith, which is not easy. In the book of Joel, God tells the elders to proclaim to the nation that a time of fasting and mourning is in order to revive the nation from their suffering. In Joel 2:13–28, God says that when we "rend our hearts and not our garments," He will pour out His Spirit on all people.

During the revival of Pentecost, Peter cites this passage from Joel in Acts 2:17–21, proclaiming that what was occurring was exactly what God said He would do as His people sought Him with all their hearts. He would "pour out my Spirit on all flesh" as a deluge of grace and conviction on all people. And then Peter proclaims in verse 33 that this is exactly what is happening to them as God is pouring out His Holy Spirit on them. Being "cut to the heart" as their hearts were rendered before God, they proclaimed, "Brothers, what shall we do?" Peter tells them to repent and be baptized, and 3,000 were converted that day. This was not Peter convincing people to repent and accept Christ through eloquent words, but God pouring out His Spirit upon the crowd, rending their hearts for repentance. All of this occurred because of the upper room, where they prayed for God's Spirit to come and bring power and conviction. It is easy to proclaim truth, but much harder to pray for it. Yet no crop will grow if the soil is not tilled first. Prayer brings the Holy Spirit, which ignites conviction in the heart of man.

> **A revival cannot occur without the Holy Spirit. Revival is a description of what has occurred, not what will happen.**

All revivals have a profound impact on the individuals, churches, and culture of that time. This impact is due to the work of the Holy Spirit. A revival cannot occur without the Holy Spirit. Revival is a description of what has occurred, not what will happen. As I stated earlier, it is laughable when a church puts out a sign advertising that they are having a "Revival Meeting" the following week. A revival is not a car show. You don't advertise it. That is like saying that I am going to a baseball game to watch a no-hitter before the game even starts. You can say you are going to a game hoping a no-hitter might occur, but most likely it will not. Likewise, we pray for a revival, but only God can determine if it will occur. When a revival transpires, there is no mistake about what it is because a revival is unlike any program a church can do. A church tries to simulate revivals, but they are nothing close to what a real revival accomplishes.

A real revival is a work of the Holy Spirit in response to the prayers of His people. A revival is a transformation of the soul of the individual from death to life. A person is confronted with their sin and is desperate to repent. They are confronted with the living God, just as Isaiah was when he entered the temple and saw the glory of God (Isaiah 6). There is no program in the church that can simulate this experience. Yet, churches often try and fail miserably. The challenge is no one knows when God will bring revival to the Church, so it cannot be programmed or planned for. God sends revival on His timetable. The only rule is that revival is the result of the prayers of Christians praying for transformation. If churches do not pray for revival, then it will not occur.

The tension is, it is easier to plan a revival meeting and hope something good occurs than to pray for revival and not be sure anything will occur. And if we pray, how long do we have to pray? It could be years. If I am determined to see a no-hitter, I could go to every baseball game my team plays and still not be rewarded. But if I go long enough and persevere, most likely I will experience the event. I believe the same is true of revival. If churches unite for prayer long enough, I believe God will send revival to our generation. The question is: are the sacrifice and perseverance worth the real event?

The answer is yes when you understand what the real event is like. A real revival is complete transformation of the soul. When revival broke out in Logan County, Kentucky, in June 1800, the congregation in Red River Meetinghouse were suddenly weeping and falling to the floor under the heavy conviction of the Holy Spirit. The pastor, James McGready, wrote, "A mighty effusion of God's Spirit came upon the people and the floor was soon covered with the slain and their screams for mercy pierced the heavens."[1]

During that summer, the Holy Spirit went from church to church, and thousands were saved as the Holy Spirit confronted men and women with their sins and they confessed Christ as their Savior. In the Beech Meeting House, John and William McGee preached from Acts 11:15, hundreds fell before them and pleaded for mercy, and they believe everyone who did not know Christ became a Christian that day. In Shiloh, a man was convicted by the Holy Spirit and tried to escape by going home and as he mounted his horse, he fell to the ground as though he were shot dead and arose sometime later praising God for His deliverance. In the Gasper River Church, one man started cursing the assembly; then, as he started walking away, a tree fell on top of him and he died. A group of men picked up his body and delivered it to his widow at his house.

The watershed event occurred in August 1801, when 25,000 people attended the meeting in Cane Ridge, Bourbon County, Kentucky. This was estimated to be about ten percent of the entire population west of the Appalachian Mountains. Presbyterian, Baptist, and Methodist pastors ministered together preaching and praying with the people. A Presbyterian minister, Pastor Stone, stated the following regarding this event:

> "There people were struck down powerless and lay as though they were in agonies of death, pleading for mercy and after a while they would arise and tell the wonders of redeeming love. The noise was like the roar of Niagara. The vast sea of human beings seemed to be agitated as if by a storm. Some of the people were singing, other praying, some crying for mercy. A peculiarly strange sensation came over me. My heart beat tumultuously; my knees trembled, my lips quivered, and I felt as though I must fall to the ground. The scene was indescrible."[2]

It was estimated about 3,000 people were saved during this event. But the work of the Holy Spirit not only convicted people of sin and brought them to salvation, the Spirit had a profound impact on the conscience of the entire area and their need to have a right relationship with the Lord. The impact of the Holy Spirit upon this area was summed up in a sermon in 1803 by Rev. David Rice at the Synod of Kentucky outlining some of the changes in the culture of the Western frontier that he personally observed:

- The Revival made its appearance in various places, without any extraordinary means to produce it. The first sign of the revival have been a praying spirit in the few pious people found among us.
- There is a deep heart-humbling sense of the great abominable nature, pernicious effects and deadly consequences of sin. There appears to be in them a deep mourning on account of their own sins and the sins of the careless and profane and particularly for the sin of

ingratitude to God for his many mercies; and conviction of the justice of God in condemning and punishing his offending creatures.
- They appear to have a lively and very affecting view of the infinite love of God the Father, in giving his only-begotten Son for the redemption of mankind.
- They seem to have a very deep and affecting sense of the work of precious immortal souls, ardent love to them, and an agonizing concern for their conviction, conversion, and complete salvation.
- A considerable number of individuals appear to be greatly reformed in their morals. Drunkards, profane swearers, liars, quarrelsome persons, etc., are remarkably reformed.
- A number of families, who had lived apparently without the fear of God, in folly and in vice, are now reduced to order, and are daily joining in the worship of God, reading His word, singing His praises, and offering up their supplication to the throne of grace.
- The subjects of this work appear to be very aware of the need of sanctification as well as justification, and that without holiness no man can see the Lord. To be greatly desirous that they should depart from iniquity, that the light of their holy conversion should shine before men seeing their good works, might give glory to God. A heaven of perfect purity and the full enjoyment of God appears to be the chief and ultimate object of their desire and pursuit.[3]

As stated earlier, a common misperception is to confuse the outer wrappings of revival with the gift itself. Many people assume that all revivals are identical, but not all revivals experience the emotional outpouring as just described. Revivals have different wrappings, but the gifts are always the same: repentance and salvation. Unfortunately, people often confuse the outer expression of what God has done for the person for the revival itself. Yes, there is great joy when a baby is born, but those tears are only the outer expression of the real truth that a new life has come into the world. The same is true of revival.

> **Revivals have different wrappings, but the gifts are always the same: repentance and salvation.**

The Prayer Revival of 1857 experienced little of the same external expression as the Second Great Awakening, yet the results were just as profound. This revival is referred to as the "Lay People's Revival" because there was nothing sensational about it except that the entire nation was praying. It was a movement of prayer across the United States, and repentance and conversions followed without a lot of preaching or the typical outward emotional demonstrations that are associated with a revival. The exact origin of the Prayer Revival of 1857 is disputed, as multiple churches in New York City were praying for revival that year.

But the traditional viewpoint is the revival was initiated in the North Dutch Church on Fulton Street in September 1857. Jeremiah Lanphier was handing out gospel tracts in New York City, and no one was interested in taking them. Does this sound familiar to our current generation? Lanphier did not give up and decided to have a prayer meeting. Instead of gospel tracts, he handed out an advertisement for a prayer meeting at noon. The first meeting was on September 23, and at noon, Jeremiah Lanphier was sitting by himself. I believe we all have had this experience. The question is, how long do you wait? Jeremiah chose to wait over thirty minutes sitting by himself, and at 12:30 p.m., one person showed up. By 1 p.m., there were six people praying. The following week, there were fourteen people and twenty-three the week after.[4]

Suddenly, the Financial Panic of 1857 occurred, and most of the banks in the Northeast failed, creating massive fear. Jeremiah decided to have the prayer meeting every day. By December, people were filling the Dutch Reformed Church, then the Methodist Church on John Street, and the Trinity Episcopal Church on Broadway Street. By February 1858, it was reported that every church and public hall in New York City was filled with people praying. Horace Greeley, the famous editor of the NY Tribune, sent out a reporter who raced around the city, attended twelve prayer meetings, and counted over 6,100 people praying. By March, it was reported that every church in New York City was praying every evening. The Holy Spirit was moving in power, bringing people together to pray.[5]

This landslide of prayer resulted in a tsunami of conversions. New York City had a population of 800,000, and people were being converted at a rate of 10,000 per week. It is estimated that in April–May of 1858, over 50,000 people became Christians in New York City. The Holy Spirit was so pervasive in the city of New York that an entire crew was converted on a ship as it arrived in the harbor of New York without anybody preaching to them. The Holy Spirit convicted them, and they repented. Soon, the entire country was praying together, and mass conversions followed throughout the nation.

> *"The influence of the Revival was felt everywhere in the nation. It first captured the great cities, but it also spread through every town and village and country hamlet. It swamped schools and colleges. It affected all classes regardless of condition. A Divine influence seemed to pervade the land, and men's hearts were strangely warmed by a Power that was outpoured in unusual ways. There was no fanaticism; there was remarkable unanimity of approval by religious and secular observers alike, with scarcely a critical voice heard anywhere. It seemed to many that the fruits of Pentecost had been repeated a thousandfold."*[6]

The Holy Spirit was working in miraculous ways throughout our country. In Kalamazoo, Michigan, all the churches united together for a prayer meeting. The leader of the meeting read a prayer request from a praying wife that her husband be saved. Immediately, a bulky man stood up and said, "I am that man; I have a praying wife and that request is for me. I want you to pray for me." As soon as he sat down, another man arose, ignoring the first man, and started crying, saying, "I am that man; I have a praying wife. She prays for me. I am sure I am that man; I want you to pray for me." Five other men stood up, one at a time, and all were converted. A spirit of conviction fell on the meeting, and 500 people were converted.[7]

In Charleston, South Carolina, which was the heart of the Confederacy, Dr. John Girardo, pastor of the Anniston Presbyterian Church, was having a prayer meeting with about sixty people, and the elders wanted him to preach, but he refused. As he was praying, he was struck in the head with a sensation that felt like a bolt of lightning and diffused through his entire body. He just sat there silently and finally got up and tried to end the service, saying he would preach the next day, but no one moved. He then realized that everyone had just had the same experience. Next, he began to hear slight sobbing that grew around him until there was a wave of emotion. They would meet every night for the following eight weeks with close to 2,000 in attendance and experienced many conversions each night.[8]

A second mistake for the church is to try to mimic the work of the Holy Spirit by relying upon a program and bypass the necessity of prayer. In 1899, the Methodist church, in anticipation of the new millennium, raised $20 million with the hope of winning two million people to Christ. It was a lofty goal, and they believed with all their new programs, they had figured out how people would come to Christ. So, after spending all the money, they had very few results. The new millennium came and went, and the church was not affected. One of the people involved said, "God waited until we got our project out of the way until He sent revival." Revival would come four years later, but only after the churches decided to make prayer a priority and prayed together continually for revival. The truth is, it is easier to spend money than pray, but prayer is the only answer to the results we are seeking. May God rend our hearts to know that we desperately need Him to pour out His Spirit on all our churches.[9]

As I learned the hard way, without gas in my car, it will not start. Everything else can be working perfectly, but gas or battery power is an absolute necessity for a car to start and take you to your destination. The same with the Holy Spirit and revival. There is no revival without the powerful working of the Holy Spirit. Just like a car, everything can be working perfectly in your church, but without power, you have no transformational results. But we can fool ourselves into thinking that our programming can substitute for the required power. Of course, this is ludicrous, but if we look at the time and energy spent on our programming in the church versus the time praying, what is the conclusion?

CHAPTER 4

PRAYER IGNITES REVIVAL

Prayer does not fit us for the greater work. Prayer is the greater work.

—Oswald Chambers

PRAYER IS LIKE DIETING. We love the results but hate the process. Who loves to diet and exercise? Most people feel the same about prayer. It can be perceived as drudgery and hard work, and the outcome is usually not immediate. For many people, prayer does not come naturally or easily. It is very difficult to make it a priority because it requires faith to believe that God will answer our prayers. So often, we are only motivated to pray when we are desperate, and we feel we are out of options.

I have seen this truth numerous times in my own life. When my oldest son was having a serious health issue while in college, I was feeling quite desperate, and for many days I prayed earnestly, but the situation only got worse. Every day he was unable to eat without vomiting, and he was quickly losing weight. When he came home for spring break, my wife and I were alarmed at how much weight he had lost and how pale he looked. He was a college cross-country and track distance runner, so he did not have extra weight to lose. After weeks of conducting medical tests, which seemed like an eternity, the doctor referred him to a surgeon, believing that his gallbladder was causing the problem, so finally, surgery was scheduled. We thought our prayers had been answered, and we were relieved.

Unfortunately, the surgery had complications, and within a week after the surgery, he was unable to get off the couch without experiencing severe abdominal pain. Returning home, he was unable to function. The days became weeks, and then months went by as he lay on the couch. A cross-country and track state qualifier was now barely able to walk across the room. Another series of tests was conducted, and there were no concrete answers to the pain. I remember talking with the insurance company and breaking down into tears regarding my son's condition.

Two months later and there still was no improvement. I went outside to water my garden, and I was so overwhelmed with emotion that all color had disappeared from my vision. All the green grass and leaves were black and white. I lost my ability to see anything in color. That reality was how I felt inside. I have no idea what I was experiencing medically at that moment, but emotionally I was in complete despair. As I started to water the garden, I wept and cried out to God, "How much longer will this occur?" And God responded, "This is for My glory, and I want you to trust Me." That was the most challenging moment of my life, to trust that God was in control of the events unraveling around me. In the midst of my desperation and prayers, I did feel the presence of God and that He was in control. The truth is we pray more often when we are desperate for God to answer. And He did answer, as I will address later.

But outside of these times when we desperately need God, prayer is missing from the average Christian's life. Almost all Christians agree that prayer is important, but how many Christians pray every day? According to a survey of 7,454 Christians across twenty major cities over two years, it was discovered that less than forty percent pray every day. Among Christians aged 18–30, the percentage is less than ten percent. Of those who do pray every day, the majority pray less than one minute. When asked why they do not pray more, the most frequent response is that they are too busy.[1]

What If God Brings Revival?

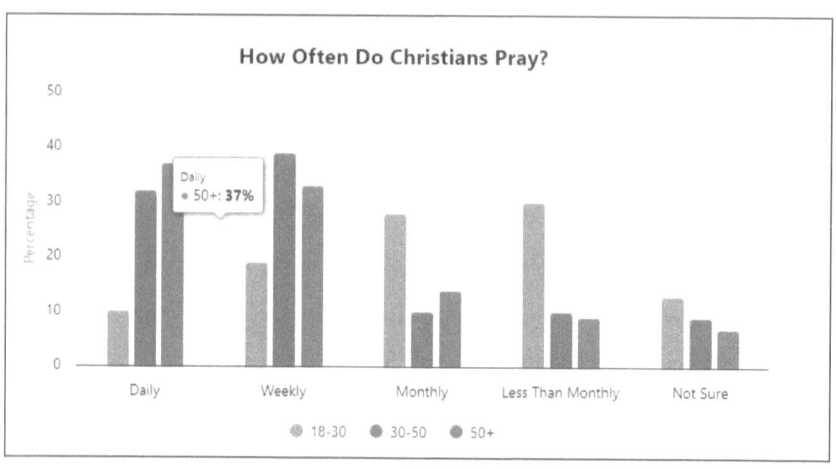

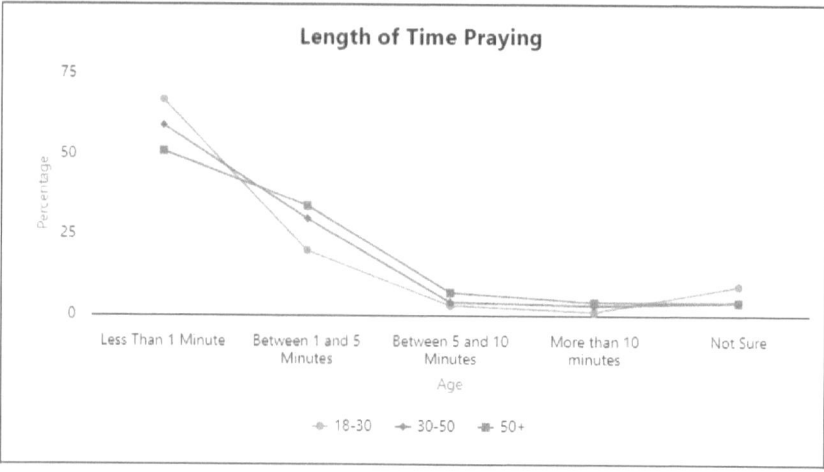

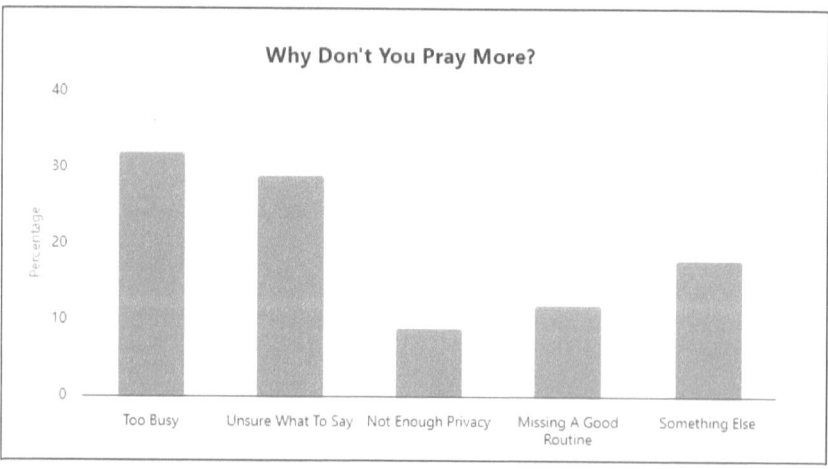

I don't think these results are shocking to anyone. All Christians know that they should be praying daily, but few do. Why? Is it that we are too busy? If so, too busy doing what? According to Statista, the average 18–24 year old in 2024 spent 186 minutes per day on social media, with TikTok being the winner at 76 minutes per day. Surprisingly, the amount of time for people over 65 was 102 minutes. The only difference was their preference for Facebook over TikTok.[2]

We all know that "too busy" is a poor excuse, as we all will do what is easiest or most enjoyable. Prayer does not fit either category. Prayer can be difficult and not the first activity we seek for enjoyment, so why would anyone do it? As a pastor, I have talked with many Christians who have wrestled with this question. Most Christians understand that they should pray more and often feel guilty for not praying. But the solution is looking at the long-term results and not seeking immediate gratification. Why does anyone go to college or trade school? Why does anyone study for an exam? Because the long-term gains outweigh the short-term pain. The key to making prayer a priority is seeing the long-term gains, and this requires faith that God will answer our prayers.

A primary reason prayer is difficult is that God rarely answers our prayers immediately. God tells us to keep knocking on the door. He tests our faith and perseverance. Do we believe that He hears us and that He will respond? I call it the microwave popcorn dilemma. When you put microwave popcorn into the microwave, the package says that it takes three minutes for the popcorn to pop. What happens if you put it in the microwave for two minutes and remove it? Nothing! Do you get two-thirds of the corn to pop? No, you get nothing. You see, it does not pop gradually, but pops suddenly, almost unexpectedly. Just when you are about to give up, it happens spontaneously.

The same with prayer. Jesus told us to pray incessantly, to keep knocking on the door until God answers. The problem is we want instant gratification. If God loves us, then why does He not open the door? So, prayer can be frustrating because we never know when God will answer. God is developing us in the process of learning to depend upon Him and to have intimacy with Him and not just getting what we want the moment we ask for it. Yes, it can be frustrating, but God is seeking to create dependence and intimacy with Him. The truth is God knows the perfect time to answer our prayers, and it rarely is on our timetable. So, the challenge is, are we willing to go deeper with Christ in prayer or do something else that seems more enjoyable and is easier to do?

> **The truth is God knows the perfect time to answer our prayers, and it rarely is on our timetable. So, the challenge is, are we willing to go deeper with Christ in prayer or do something else that seems more enjoyable and is easier to do?**

Why should we pray? Prayer requires the belief that God not only hears our prayers but will answer them. And His answer makes the sacrifice of prayer worthwhile. In other words, the result of the answered prayer is worth the effort of praying, even when very little has been seen.

Every revival is different, but there is one characteristic that is true of every revival that ever occurred. Every revival is the result of people praying together, sometimes for several years. A major problem is we have unrealistic expectations. We want God to answer our prayers immediately. I believe this is natural for everyone, but more so for Americans, where we value instant gratification. But the benefits need to be considered when we weigh out the costs.

The Second Great Awakening was ignited by people committed to praying together for over two years without first seeing any results. Rev. Isaac Backus was motivated by a book written by Jonathan Edwards regarding the necessity of unified and extraordinary prayer required for a revival to occur, and he sent a letter in 1794 to every Christian denomination calling for a "Concert of Prayer." The Presbyterians in New Jersey and Pennsylvania adopted it along with the Methodists and Baptists and Congregationalists.[3]

The entire East Coast was a network of prayer meetings in which the first Monday of each month was dedicated to prayer. They prayed for two years when suddenly revival broke out in Connecticut and then to Massachusetts and swept down to New York and then to Philadelphia as churches in each of these areas had been praying. Their perseverance was rewarded as the Awakening ignited the church and many people confessed and thousands were saved. The Spirit moved in power, but with a quiet conviction that brought thousands to repentance. Young people would be in the tavern or on the dance floor and suddenly would feel convicted by the Spirit and would leave seeking spiritual counsel.[4]

The Second Great Awakening then leaped across the Appalachian Mountains in 1800 due to the efforts of James

McGready and several hundred people praying for revival. In 1796, James McGready was called by God to leave his church in North Carolina and to move to Logan County, Kentucky, to pastor three churches: Muddy River, Red River, and Gasper River churches. Logan County was also known as "Rogue's Harbor." This was the place where fugitives escaped to when they committed a crime on the East Coast and the law was chasing them. There was no law in this area and the criminals ran the place. Matter of fact, it is claimed that the citizens tried to form a vigilante group to arrest the fugitives and were defeated.[5]

James McGready was not naïve of where he was going, but he believed that God had a great plan for this area. But before he left, he got several hundred people from multiple churches to commit to pray for Logan County and the three churches. Everyone signed a covenant that they would pray for the conversion of Logan County the third Saturday of each month and also would pray for James McGready for thirty minutes at sunset on Saturday evening and sunrise on Sunday morning. They committed that they would pray until either God bought revival or they died! That is called open-ended prayer![6]

> **They committed that they would pray until either God bought revival or they died! That is called open-ended prayer!**

The year 1797 came and went and nothing happened, but the people kept praying. James McGready wrote in his diary in that the winter of 1798 was for the most part "weeping and mourning with the people of God."[7] Lawlessness prevailed everywhere. The people in North Carolina kept praying. The first sign of revival occurs in July 1799 in the Red River Church in which the Holy Spirit came and dozens of people begin confessing sin and are lying on the floor stricken by the power of the Holy Spirit. Then it went quiet again.

But then eleven months later, the Holy Spirit returns with a fervor as hundreds of people are converted as the Spirit moves in power through Logan County. In June, 1800 at the Red River Meetinghouse, the meeting is about to close when the visiting minister, William McGee, says, "Let the Lord God Omnipotent reign in your hearts!" Suddenly, the Spirit moved and waves of people begin weeping and others falling to the floor under the deep conviction of sin. James McGready, who was observing the crowd, later wrote, "A mighty effusion of God's Spirit came upon the people and the floor was soon covered with the slain and their screams for mercy pierced the heavens."[8] When the revival continues in the states of Kentucky and Tennessee, it is no longer a quiet revival, but one that accompanies great emotion from those who are filled with His presence.

I wonder what they were thinking when they signed this covenant. Were they insane? The idea of revival coming to these three little churches in Kentucky was lunacy. And the group was tested because they prayed for three years with no results. How many of us would agree to such terms and be willing to pray faithfully for three years with no results? But desperation and faith motivated these committed Christians to pray. God will not bring revival to our churches and our country without prayer. Often, we are not honest about how little we pray. Every revival was the result of extraordinary prayer that occurred in the church for an extended period of time.

> **Every revival was the result of extraordinary prayer that occurred in the church for an extended period of time.**

But how can we motivate people to pray more and to believe that God will bring revival? In past revivals, there was a sense of desperation that unless God answers, there was no hope. I think one advantage the Christians had when they prayed for revival was, they remembered what God had done in the prior generation. The greatest revivals in our history occurred about 40–50 years apart and thus many people were still alive who had personally witnessed the great revival that had occurred in the previous generation. I believe this personal experience was the motivation they had to organize the churches together and pray corporately with a fervency and desperation because they saw what God had done and they wanted it again!

There is no substitute for personal experience. In my lifetime, I experienced the first and second Gulf Wars and 9/11 but did not experience World War II. For most of us, 9/11 was a real event that we all lived through. And every one of us has a personal story of exactly where we were when we heard the news of the Twin Towers falling on that dreadful day. We not only remember the event, but how we felt and the feelings of disbelief. For us who lived through it, it was not only a historical event, but it was an emotional journey. I personally was stranded at the St. Louis airport that morning as I was in transit between flights. The feeling of shock and despair as I searched desperately through mounds of luggage from hundreds of flights that were suddenly grounded in St. Louis is still very real for me. But for my daughter who was born after 9/11, she only knows it as a historical event. She can give you the details of what occurred, but she did not experience the shock, disbelief, and despair many of us felt on that day.

Likewise, I did not live through World War II and the many horrific events that occurred from 1939–1945. I have heard many of the stories. I lived in Poland for a while, and our landlords survived the atrocities of a concentration camp and still had the numbers that were tattooed on their arms. They personally experienced the horror of hell from the Nazis and their memories are filled with emotions that I can never understand. We now live in a generation where the savagery of World War II is long forgotten, even to the point that some people like to claim that the concentration camps never occurred. This revisionist history can only occur with people who did not actually experience the terrors of these camps or personally know someone who did. It is much easier to deny reality when you only read it in a history book. But those who lived through the First and Second World Wars refer to them as the "Great Wars" with the commitment that they should never occur again.

Likewise, many of the people who prayed for the Great Revivals personally experienced a previous revival. It was not just a historical event, but it was an experience that they personally witnessed and they longed for it to occur again. I believe this was a great motivation for them to both pray and believe that God would do what He had already done in their lifetime. They had witnessed how the Holy Spirit brought many people to repent of their sins and to accept Christ as their Savior. They saw how people prayed throughout the night in the churches and worshipped God. They saw how stores closed and businesses stopped for pray, not because they had to, but they wanted to. They saw how churches doubled in size and thousands were converted. They witnessed how the culture was changed and suddenly everyone was going to church and believing in Christ was the norm. There is no substitute for personal experience.

Unfortunately, we have not had the privilege of experiencing what they witnessed. Our only knowledge is in history books, and though the stories are amazing, we did not experience it firsthand. But can we believe that God did an amazing work in our previous generations and that the history we read is historical facts that occurred? If God sent His Spirit in power as a result of corporate prayer, will He do it again? Are we desperate enough to see God move in power? We need to not only appreciate the history, but to try to live it. To hear the stories as if we are sitting on the knee of our grandparents as they tell us what they experienced. To allow the stories to permeate our consciousness and move our emotions to embrace it as not only truth but a reality that will move us to action. To pray corporately with a fervor believing that what God has done in the past, He will do again. The challenge is we cannot give up when nothing happens. We must commit to the work and perseverance that prayer demands. God will test our faith in Him. We must remember the stories and believe that God will do it again. We must promise to pray corporately until God responds, regardless of how long it takes.

In the First Great Awakening, Jonathan Edwards wrote a book whose title feels longer than the book itself: *A Humble Attempt to Promote Explicit Agreement and Visible Union of all God's People in Extraordinary Prayer for the Revival of Religion and the Advancement of Christ's Kingdom on earth pursuant to Scripture Promises and Prophecies concerning the last time.* The book promoted unified and extraordinary prayer across denominational lines that was focused on revival. This meant that the prayer was more than just a couple of minutes a day; it enabled the people praying to enter into the presence of God and petition before the throne for God to send revival. It does not mean that your entire life is rearranged but that it is one of the priorities in your life. Sadly, very few Christians pray more than a couple of minutes a day, which is very ordinary at best. Every revival requires a period of time in which the people are praying in unity and agreement that God will pour out His Spirit in power. The prayer is not just a quick nod to the Lord but a focused effort showing that this is a priority in our lives.

The history of revivals teaches us that every revival began because people focused on praying together for God to pour out His Spirit. No revival ever occurred without unified and extraordinary prayer. This means people came together as one in the Body of Christ and prayed for a period of time specifically for God to send revival. Then, they continued to pray for a period of months and sometimes years with this focus. In I John 5:14, God tells us that if we ask for anything according to His will, He hears us, and we know that we will have what we asked for. How could repentance and salvation of many people not be God's will? This is God's will, and He is greatly pleased when we make it priority and pray for it over a period of time. The key to revival is make something that is not natural or easy a priority in our lives, because the outcome is worth the sacrifice.

Going back to the experience with my oldest son and his health issues, desperation drove my motivation for prayer. God had spoken to me, but my son was still on his back unable to function. But the following week, I was in my office working when I suddenly heard a basketball bouncing on our driveway. I jumped up and ran to the window to see my son shooting hoops. Tears rolled down my cheeks. That was the first sign of hope I had for months. Several weeks later, he returned to college for his senior year, and he was back on the cross-country team running again. It was a miracle! And God was glorified in that my son was redirected through this event in his life to become a teacher and has now been teaching science overseas in Christian International Schools. Yes, God was glorified and answered my prayers through my desperation.

This is the desperation that conceives the mighty prayers of the saints to unleash the power of the Holy Spirit on His Church. Revival is a wonderful event, and we should seek it with all our hearts and not be afraid of it, whether it is for one person or an entire nation. Revival is a miracle that is the result of the Church praying and believing that God will be exalted. (A Great Revival has not occurred for over a hundred years in America. Though there have been many small revivals and ones that definitely impacted large groups of people, we have not experienced a Great revival that sweeps the entire nation since the Welsh revival came to America.) By understanding the power of revival and God's heart, may we embrace revival and believe that God wants to do in our generation what He has done for previous generations as they prayed fervently for it to occur. Would we be willing to follow in the footsteps of our forefathers to sign a covenant that they would pray for revival until God brought revival or they died? This is not a light decision, but one based on commitment and perseverance. It recognizes that prayer is hard work but believes that God will honor the work of prayer and will send revival when we pray for it.

At the beginning of the chapter, I mentioned that prayer is like dieting. A few years ago, I was convinced that I needed to lose a few pounds. Well, not just a few, but thirty pounds. This was before taking a pill was an option, so I committed to jogging fifteen miles every week and tracking my calories so that I did not eat more than 1500 calories in any day. I am not a nutritionist, so I am not advocating this plan for you, but as I committed to it, I found that I achieved results. I lost about two pounds every week following this plan. Was it difficult at time? Absolutely! Did I want to run two-three miles almost every day? No! But perseverance and commitment paid off! Then, people started to notice which encouraged me even more. Prayer and dieting and exercise all require commitment and perseverance, but they also all provide wonderful results. Our physical bodies reap the benefits of dieting and exercise. But prayer delivers benefits for eternity, and it changes not only our lives but the lives of many people.

CHAPTER 5

WHY CORPORATE PRAYER?

The early church prayed. Every revival church has prayed. Every participant in revival prayer has known travail. Though there are some tearful intercessors behind the scenes, I grant you that to our modern Christianity, praying is foreign.

—Leonard Ravenhill,
Revival Praying: An Urgent and Powerful Message for the Family of Christ

A FEW YEARS AGO, OUR church purchased a furniture store to convert it into a church. One of the tasks involved was the clearing of a small forest of trees that would become the church parking lot. As the large trees were cut down, we really did not want to pay to have all the wood hauled away, so we made a massive pile of logs and branches on the property to burn. But then it occurred to me that maybe the township would not allow us to burn this wood, so I called the township office to see if burning this massive pile of logs and branches would be legal. The secretary explained to me that as long as it was a campfire for the purpose of cooking food, it would be legal. I then asked what made it a legitimate campfire. She said as long as we were cooking food, it would be considered a campfire. I asked, "So as long as we are roasting hot dogs, we would be okay?" "Yes, that would be fine." So, I went to the local grocery store and bought five packages of hot dogs, buns, and condiments.

On the next workday, I told everyone we were going to have lunch outside by roasting hot dogs. Did I mention that there was a foot of snow on the ground, and it was only ten degrees? Everyone, including myself, thought we were crazy! So, we lit the giant woodpile and suddenly realized that the heat was so overwhelming that we could not stand anywhere close to it to roast the hot dogs as an enormous bonfire shot high into the sky. We stood about thirty feet away from the flames holding metal rods about three feet long with a hot dog on the end pretending to have a campfire. This was no campfire; this was a firestorm on the edge of being out of control. Fortunately, because there was a foot of snow on the ground, no one was concerned that this fire could burn down the building 200 feet away that we were renovating. But it was a real possibility, and the larger and higher this blaze expanded, the closer it got to the building. I was sure that if the fire department arrived, we could not have convinced them that this was just a campfire to roast a few hot dogs.

The question often asked is why is corporate prayer necessary for revival? Why does Jesus say that where two or more are gathered in My Name, I am there (Mt. 18:20)? Is not God present when I pray on my own? The answer is yes, but I believe Jesus is saying that when we pray together, we are praying as the Body of Christ (the Church) on behalf of the Church to the Head of the Church, which is Jesus. And if we want revival to come to our church, the prayers should be from the Church praying together. I believe it is the same when we consider the universal Church. One overlooked fact about Great Revivals that swept across our nation is that they were all initiated by the universal Church praying together for the purpose of revival over an extended period of time. I do not know of one example where a revival occurred without Christians being united together praying for it.

> **I believe that nothing pleases God more than when His Church is praying together across all denominations for the repentance, healing, and revival of the Church.**

I believe that nothing pleases God more than when His Church is praying together across all denominations for the repentance, healing, and revival of the Church. Yes, the prayer of a righteous man is powerful and effective, as we read in James 5:16, as it pertains to confession and healing, but the prayers of thousands of righteous men and women can create a firestorm. God is honored when the Church is united as One Body for the purpose of praying for His Will. It is no coincidence that the Second Great Awakening was ignited by the prayers of many denominations praying together fervently and consistently. The letter that Isaac Backus sent to every Christian leader of every denomination to pray for healing and repentance was critical in igniting the firestorm that changed the face of the nation.

But if personal praying is difficult, corporate praying seems almost impossible in many churches. Announcing a prayer meeting typically does not receive a jubilant response. It often is a small group of older saints gathered together in a small room. Of course, there are exceptions to this, but most churches really struggle to make corporate prayer a priority. This is tragic because corporate prayer should be the main dish of the Church and not just an appetizer that is considered optional.

> **Corporate prayer unifies the parts of the body to each other and to the Head, Jesus, in perfect harmony to hear from Him and to respond in unison to His will.**

When you pray together as a church, there is a fire ignited within the soul of the Church that soon becomes contagious. The more people who pray together, the easier and more powerful prayer becomes. Corporate prayer unifies the parts of the body to each other and to the Head, Jesus, in perfect harmony to hear from Him and to respond in unison to His will. The problem is the initiation of the prayer can be difficult, just like trying to start a fire on a wet, cold day. People are distracted and have other priorities in their lives. Prayer is rarely a top priority, even for the most mature Christian. So how do we motivate people to pray together?

My friend, Dayle Keefer, who pastored for forty-five years, told me that he learned from Jim Cymbala that corporate prayer is a priority in the Church when it is the only option in the Church. In other words, people will make it a priority when all other options are eliminated. He said that on Wednesday nights at the church he pastored, the only activity they did was pray. You have to believe that corporate prayer is a priority that will reap wonderful benefits to make this decision. It is helpful to keep track and celebrate together when God answers our prayers. Though prayers are not always answered immediately, they are answered, and often we fail to see the answers because we do not keep track of the prayers and thus fail to see what God has done.

Corporate prayer in the Church is wonderful as you pray for the congregation and the community, and you can see incredible things happen. But as you unite churches together in your community, you are throwing more logs on the fire, and that fire grows as God is glorified with the unity in His Church. When I was pastoring in Nebraska, there was a rundown barn that was called Satan's Coven and was known in the area as the place to go for entertainment in the fall. Long lines would form as people paid to walk through the "haunted" place to be entertained and scared.

Our church felt that this place was an obstacle to the proclamation of the gospel in our town, and so we prayed that God would intervene. God then gave me the idea of uniting all the churches and walking together as "March For Jesus" in the Fourth of July parade. There were several hundred of us walking together, waving our Jesus banners and singing, and handing out candy. Meanwhile, we were all praying about this building as we walked by it. The next day, the building caught on fire and burned to the ground. It ended the haunted fall festivities for the city, and we praised the Lord. I believe the Lord brought literal fire to the building because all the churches in our town were united in praying for the city.

Jesus was clear to His disciples that they were to pray together in Jerusalem and wait for the Holy Spirit. He was explicit that they should not leave Jerusalem but should pray corporately, waiting for the Lord to work. He promised that when the Holy Spirit came in power, then they would be His witnesses throughout Jerusalem, Judea, Samaria, and to the ends of the earth. They returned to Jerusalem and went to the upstairs room where they joined together constantly in prayer. They persevered in prayer together, encouraging each other to be patient, waiting for the promise of the Spirit that Jesus had given them. By trusting God, they made corporate prayer the priority and believed that God would bring the power to be His witnesses as He told them in Acts 1:8.

Suddenly, the Spirit came to the entire group praying with the sound of a violent wind, and the Holy Spirit filled each one present in the room. And suddenly, they went from being fearful disciples questioning their future to powerful men and women of God filled with the Holy Spirit, boldly proclaiming the gospel throughout Jerusalem and performing miracles to the point that at the end of Peter's opening sermon, three thousand were added to the church on the first day.

It is easy to excuse what occurred in the New Testament as an extraordinary event that God performed for the purpose of beginning His church. But history tells us differently. Throughout history, including this past century, we have the church being ignited and growing in a country because a group of people prayed earnestly together for God to send His Spirit. Revivals have occurred in many parts of the world, not just in the USA and Great Britain. Most people know that one of the largest Christian churches exists in South Korea. The growth of the church can be attributed to the Great Pyongyang Revival of 1907, also known as the "Korean Pentecost," which dramatically changed the landscape of the church in Korea. In the early 20th century, pastors and missionaries across different denominations united in prayer and repentance, seeking divine guidance. On the day that the Holy Spirit came, Mr. Lee gives the following personal account:

> *On the Monday at noon, we missionaries met and cried out to God in earnest. We were bound in spirit and refused to let God go till He blessed us. That night it was very different. Each felt as he entered the church that the room was full of God's presence. Not only missionaries but Koreans testify to the same thing. I was present once in Wisconsin when the Spirit of God fell upon a company of lumbermen and every unbeliever in the room rose to ask for prayers. That night in Pyeng Yang, the same feeling came to me as I entered the*

room, a feeling of God's nearness, impossible of description. After a short sermon, I took charge of the meeting and called for prayers. So many began praying and I said, "If you want to pray like that, all pray," and the whole audience began to pray out loud all together. The effect was indescribable. Not confusion, but a vast harmony of sound and spirit, a mingling together of souls moved by an irresistible impulse of prayer. The prayer sounded to me like the falling of many waters, an ocean of prayer beating against God's throne. It was not many, but one, born of one Spirit, lifted to one Father above. Just as on the day of Pentecost, they were all together in one place, of one accord praying, "and suddenly there came from heaven the sound as of the rushing of a mighty wind, and it filled all the house where they were sitting." God is not always in the whirlwind, neither does He always speak in a still small voice. He came to us in Pyeng Yang that night with the sound of weeping. As the prayer continued, a spirit of heaviness and sorrow for sin came down upon the audience. Over on one side, someone began to weep, and in a moment the whole audience was weeping[1]

The revival quickly spread across the nation, characterized by fervent prayer meetings that would last through the night. People of all ages and backgrounds came together, praying for personal renewal, societal transformation, and unity among the churches. The impact was profound, leading to a rapid expansion of the Christian faith across Korea. Churches grew exponentially, and the movement laid the groundwork for what would become one of the largest Christian populations in Asia. All of this was due to missionaries and pastors across multiple denominations uniting together in corporate prayer, believing that God would do a mighty work in Korea.

One question that is often asked about revival is why it often does not spread from one location to another. In the past decade, there have been several significant revivals that have occurred in our country and made a meaningful impact on the school or church where it occurred. People even come from surrounding areas to be able to participate in the revival, but it eventually dies out without spreading across the country. The Asbury Revival that started in February of 2023 and lasted several months is a prime example. When this revival broke out, thousands of people traveled to Asbury University to experience the revival. It had a profound impact on the campus and on the many people who came to experience it, but the revival never traveled across the country as previous revivals did. A key difference is that prayer for the revival was concentrated only in that area and was not unified across the nation involving the universal Church.

In previous revivals, when revival breaks out, people in other areas are already praying for revival or soon organize the efforts in their respective cities and towns and begin to pray for revival for their area. By praying, they were chopping down trees and making their own stacks of wood for the Holy Spirit to be poured out upon and ignite a blaze in their area. In each of the Great Revivals, the revival spread like a fire from one area to another, but not randomly. It spread from east to west as people in each area were praying for God to pour out His Spirit. In more recent revivals, people from surrounding areas have traveled to the revival, but large groups of people in surrounding states were not praying that God would pour out His Spirit in their location. They were not piling the wood for God to send His fire upon their land.

In the Great Revival of 1857, it was reported that a man from Omaha showed up in Boston for a prayer meeting that Charles Finney was having, and he stated that the route was one continuous prayer meeting as the entire country was praying for revival.[2] When revival broke out in New York City in the fall of 1857, everyone did not flock to New York City to see what was occurring, but instead, they organized prayer meetings in each of their towns so that the entire nation was praying, seeking a revival.

This was laying down the wood across our nation so the revival could spread down the East Coast and then westward throughout 1858, engulfing the entire nation in the fire of the Holy Spirit. The initiation of a Great Revival not only depends upon corporate prayer across denominational lines but also across geography so that the entire Church is praying in all locations for revival. So, when the revival starts in a particular location, the stage is set for the revival to go from town to town as people have been praying.

When the Great Welsh Revival came to America in 1905, people across the country were praying for revival in their city. Yale College reported that one-quarter of the student body was attending daily prayer meetings. In Atlanta, over 1,000 businesspeople were praying daily. In Burlington, Iowa, every store and factory closed their doors for prayer from 10–11 a.m. In January 1906, the mayor called for a day of prayer, and all the schools and stores closed and 12,000 prayed together in the churches. When the revival swept across America to the West Coast, two hundred stores in Portland and Seattle signed an agreement to close daily from 11 a.m.–2 p.m. for prayer. In Los Angeles, one hundred churches came together and reported that over 180,000 people attended prayer meetings.³

The goal is not to seek the sensational, but to understand the importance of corporate prayer in seeking God together. There is no guarantee when or how God will answer our prayers when we cry out to Him, but there is a guarantee that nothing will occur if we choose not to pray. Unfortunately, choosing not to pray is the easy choice. Choosing to pray requires faith that God will answer in His timetable. It is God's desire to see revival occur in the Church leading to repentance and salvation of many souls. Corporate, united prayer has always ignited a movement of God and the pouring out of His Spirit. We have the Bible and history to encourage our faith, but we still have to make the choice to make prayer a priority above all other choices. What we choose corporately has a dramatic impact on the health and growth of the Church.

When I almost succeeded in burning down our new church building, as I described at the beginning of this chapter, I learned a very simple lesson: the amount of wood determines the extent of the fire. In my desire to be efficient, thinking I could pile an entire forest together in one massive pile and burn it together, I almost succeeded in burning down our church and maybe the city in the process. Fortunately, I am sure the cold weather and snow on the ground kept me from explaining to the fire chief the lame excuse that we were only having a campfire. But when it comes to revival, corporate prayer that is unified and extraordinary across a large geographical area and denominational lines will create a firestorm of revival that cannot be controlled. This should be our motivation for God to pour out His Spirit on our land.

CHAPTER 6

REVIVAL BRINGS CHANGE TO THE CHURCH

A revival is not the Church deciding to do something and doing it. It is something that is *done* to the Church, something that happens to the Church.

—Martyn Lloyd Jones

MY WIFE AND I were missionaries in Poland, and we had the privilege of visiting many churches filled with people who loved the Lord, often meeting in rundown buildings that were very unattractive. When we returned to the USA, one of the things that shocked us was the amount of money churches in the USA spend on their buildings. One church I visited had escalators throughout the building and elaborate glass spires. When you consider the amount of money spent on buildings, you would assume that the quality of the buildings is one of the primary reasons a person would decide to go to a particular church. Another unique thing about the American church that surprised me was the myriad of programs offered for every age group. Again, you would assume that this must be one of the primary reasons a person would select one church to attend versus another.

> **But when Americans are asked the question of why they attend church, the overwhelming response is very simple: to be closer to God.**

But when Americans are asked the question of why they attend church, the overwhelming response is very simple: to be closer to God. People genuinely want to experience the presence of God when they attend worship services. The attractiveness of a church is equated to whether the presence of God is experienced. The more people experience God, the more fulfilled they will be, and, more likely, they will invite others to attend. It really could not be any simpler. If you want more people to come to your church, you should desire that the presence of God is there. The only problem is that the presence of God is not dependent upon the building, the programs, or the service itself. The presence of God is strictly dependent upon the Holy Spirit being poured out on the Church. So, is it any surprise when we look back at history and see that attendance at churches dramatically increases when the Holy Spirit is powerfully present in our sanctuaries?

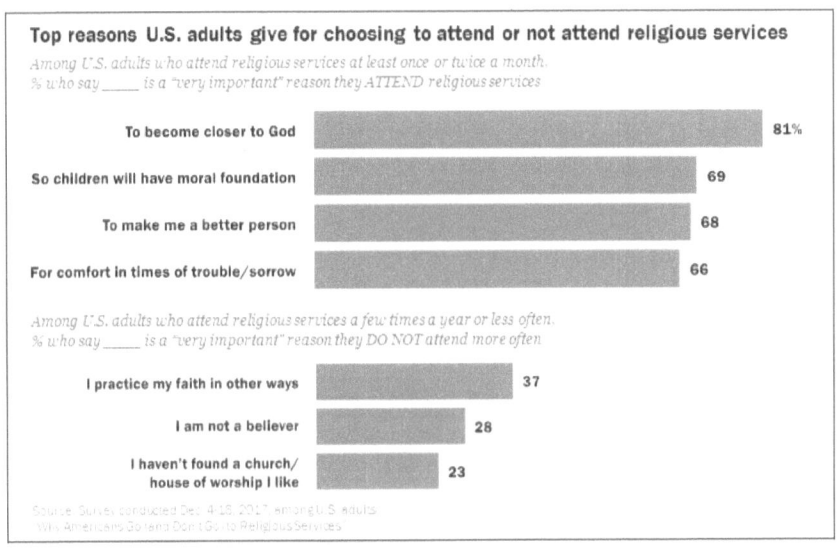

https://www.pewresearch.org/religion/2018/08/01/
why-americans-go-to-religious-services[1]

There is a real irony in that we spend substantial amounts of money and effort on trying to figure out ways to get people to visit our churches. Yet, there is a significant decline in people attending church in the 21st century. The drop in church attendance is down for all ages, but most notably for Millennials (36 percent) and Generation Z (16 percent). It has also dropped for every demographic, including gender, race, education, party affiliation, and geographic location. There is not one subset of our population in the USA that is attending church more than they were twenty years ago. These percentages include all faiths, but when you only consider Christian faiths, the trend is similar, with evangelicals dropping from 26.3 percent in 2007 to 25.4 percent in 2014. (The only exception to this trend is non-denominational churches, in which 6.5 million more people attend in 2020 than in 2010 in the USA, according to a 2020 US Religion Census).[2]

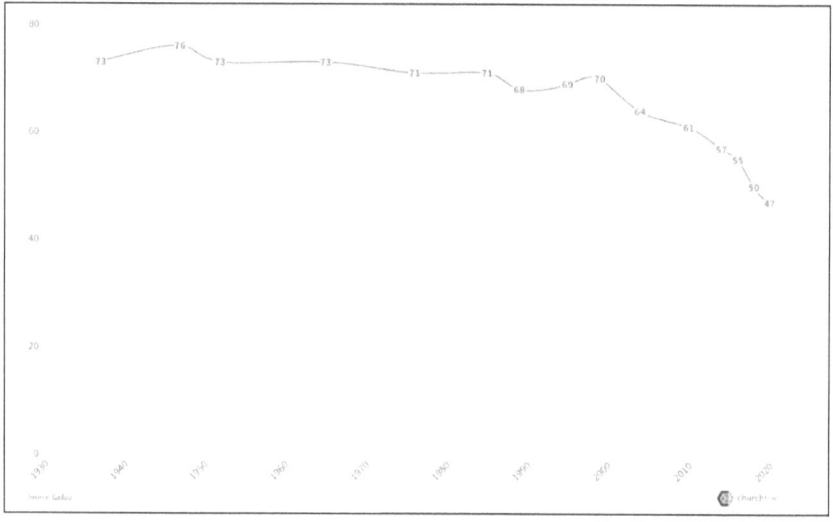

https://www.churchtrac.com/articles/the-state-of-church-membership#:~:text=What%20Percentage%20of%20Americans%20are,a%20decline%20since%20that%20year.[3]

Revival Brings Change to the Church

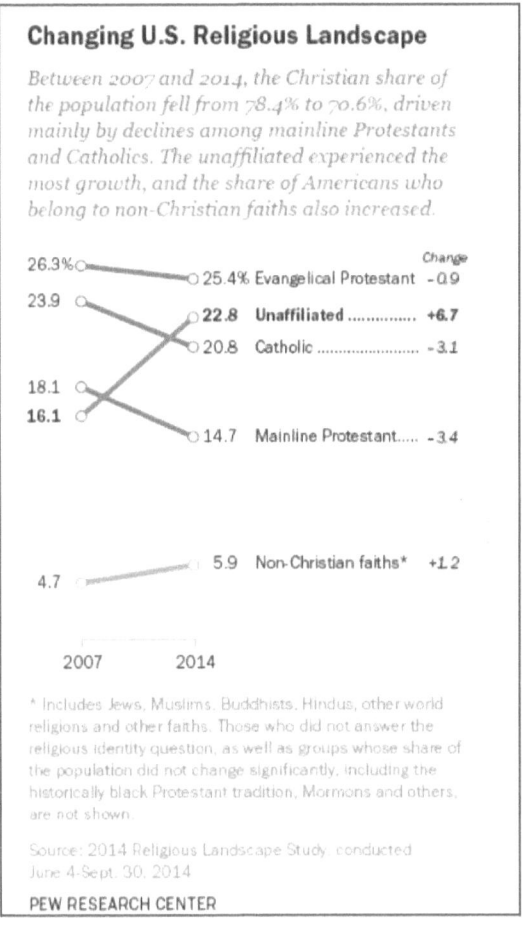

https://www.pewresearch.org/religion/2015/05/12/
americas-changing-religious-landscape[4]

What is really alarming is the percentage of people who claim to belong to a church that never attend church. From 2000 to 2022, this number has increased from 13 percent to 31 percent whereas the number that do attend every week has dropped significantly from 32 percent to 20 percent. This means that only 1/5 of those people who claim to be part of church actually attend church every Sunday.

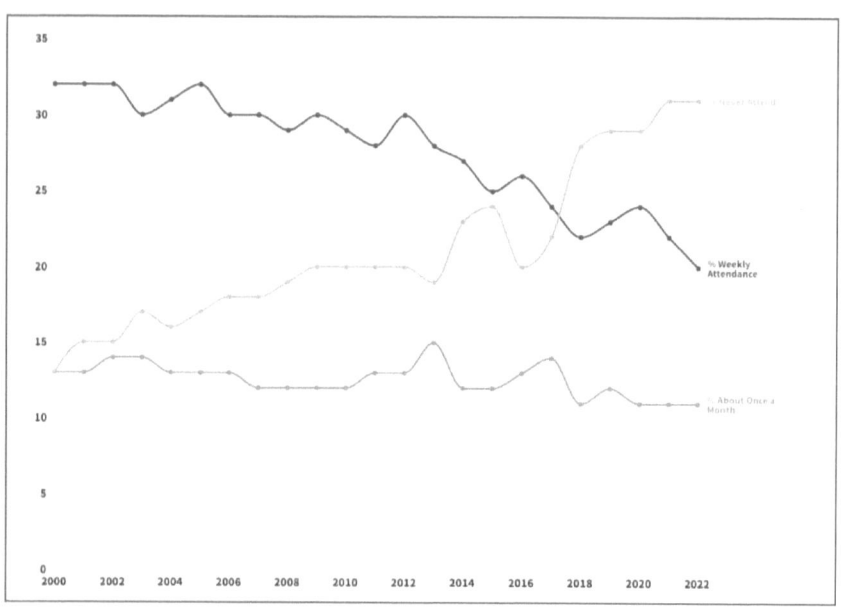

https://www.churchtrac.com/articles/
the-state-of-church-attendance-trends-and-statistics-2023[5]

How has church attendance varied throughout our history and what has been the primary motivation for people to attend church? Most people view the 1700s as a time when America was very religious and thus will often state that we were founded as a "Christian nation." If you base this statement solely on church attendance in the early 1700s, this would be true because church attendance was primarily an obligation in which everyone in the community was required to participate, regardless of personal conviction, so church attendance was significantly higher. When the First Great Awakening occurred and many people were saved, suddenly there was a large movement of people who wanted to belong to a church where the attendees had been truly transformed by the Holy Spirit.

In 1741, when Isaac Backus was converted, he returned to his parish church but found no comfort from the preaching and no reinforcement from the congregation that included many unconverted people. When he and others who had been transformed asked the minister to exclude from membership those who experientially did not know Christ, the minister refused, and so they left the church and formed a "Separate church," meeting in a private home. In 1756, Backus left the "Separate" church to form a "Separate Baptist" church. By 1755, there were 125 Separatist churches in New England, and by 1776, there were an additional seventy Separatist Baptist churches. The Separatist movement created a great upheaval in the colonial period as people now had choices to attend church or not attend, or even better, to attend a church that they felt was filled with people who had been transformed. Edwin Gaustad commented that the First Great Awakening destroyed the "traditional parish system, weakened the structure of the establishment, and undermined the Saybrook Platform, which attempted to unite the church and state".[6] As a result, the entrenched power of the established Congregational church in New England was undermined, and dissent could no longer be held in check.

Unlike other revivals, the First Great Awakening did not greatly increase church attendance, but it did transform the church. Before the Awakening, church attendance was primarily a civic duty and not a personal conviction. But the Awakening not only reorganized the established church but changed the motives for going to church. Now people were more apt to attend church due to a personal relationship with the Lord and not due to compulsion. However, following the Awakening, church attendance began to drop in the 1760s and 1770s as people were less obligated to attend and other teachings began to compete for the heart of the new Republic. By 1776, church attendance was at seventeen percent.[7] The low point occurs in 1790 when church attendance drops to about ten percent.[8]

This does not mean that the entire population was against religion, but they were less likely to attend church unless their conversion to Christ had been genuine. There was still a belief that religion was good for society and that it upheld morals and virtues, but the notion that it was your civic duty to attend church was fading quickly. In addition, people were beginning to embrace "reason" or "common sense" as their core belief instead of "faith" due to Enlightenment thought. The anger and rebellion towards Great Britain also led to an independent and rebellious mindset that man could control his own destiny. These forces led to a sudden downturn in church attendance in the period of the 1770s–80s, leading some people to question if Christianity would even exist as we entered the 19th century. As Thomas Paine, author of *Common Sense*, boldly proclaimed, "Christianity will be dead in 30 years."[9]

But in the 18th century, a major reversal occurs, and church membership suddenly jumps from ten percent in 1790 to thirty-four percent in 1830 to 45% by 1890.[10] The height of church membership peaks right after WWII to over fifty percent before a slow decline to the present time. The 19th century was the greatest period of church growth in our entire history. So, what prompted such a reversal? Maybe the churches learned about church growth techniques, or they formed better welcoming committees, or had better children's programs? The explanation is quite simple. The Holy Spirit came in great power to our country, sweeping away all poor excuses for why they rejected God, convicting people of sin, and drawing them to Jesus. In the period between 1796 to 1920, we experienced three major revivals in the USA, each about 50 years apart and lasting for an entire generation. In other words, the Holy Spirit swept through the nation as a great tsunami, and as soon as it began to die down, another wave followed. Every generation, for a period of 120 years, experienced this incredible phenomenon of God's Spirit being poured out in great power upon the church.

The credit for these three great revivals can be given to the Christians in the early 1790s, who understood what they needed to do. Having witnessed the movement of God's Spirit only forty years prior in the First Great Awakening, these Christians did not rely upon programs or buildings to solve their problems, but prayer. As discussed in chapter four, Isaac Backus, a Baptist pastor in Connecticut, sent a letter in 1794 to every Christian leader of every Christian denomination calling for a "Concert of Prayer." Backus was seventy years old, so he had witnessed what God had done in the 1740s and wanted to see it happen again. Soon, the entire country was interlaced with a network of prayer meetings in which the first Monday of the month was set aside for prayer. For two years, nothing happened, but the churches continued to pray for revival. Personal experience is a powerful motivator to believe that something will happen, so instead of their prayer efforts dissipating, they persevered, believing that God would respond.

The Second Great Awakening erupted in 1796 in Connecticut and Massachusetts, then spread to the rest of New England, New York, and Philadelphia. Contrary to popular impressions of revivals, the revival that occurred in the eastern US was without any demonstrations but had a quiet undertone of repentance and salvation, and the results were impressive. Thousands were converted across all denominations weekly.

Within the next decade, church membership doubled across all denominations. The Methodists were the smallest of all denominations in 1776 and became the largest by the early 1800s with 1,324,000 members. The Baptists were the third largest denomination and became the second largest. Their membership rose from 95,000 in 1800 to 815,000. In the state of Connecticut, there had been fifty-nine Baptist churches in 1800 with 4,600 members, and by 1820, the number rose to seventy-three churches with 7,500 members, and to eighty-three by 1830 with 9,200 members.[11] The churches that gained the most members were the most evangelistic in word and action and the most suited to a democratic government. The Baptists and Methodists experienced the greatest number of salvations of all the denominations.

When Joshua Marsden, a British Methodist Minister, visited the USA in 1802, he stated, *"I cannot contemplate without astonishment the great work that God has performed in the United States. It is here we see Methodism it its grandest form. In England, Methodism is like a river calmly guiding on; here it is a torrent, rushing along and sweeping all away in its course."* God had answered the prayers of Isaac Backus, the most prominent of the Baptist pastors in Connecticut.[12]

But the results were even more impressive west of the Appalachian Mountains. Due to the great efforts of the people who signed the North Carolina Covenant and prayed for Logan County for over three years until God brought a great revival to their area, the churches exploded in attendance beginning in 1800. People came from everywhere and were converted. One small church, Beach Street Church, had 500 people accept Christ in the summer of 1800 and 125 became new members. In another small church, Gasper River Church, over 8,000 people came from over 100 miles to hear the gospel. The watershed event was the revival meeting in Cane Ridge, Bourbon County, Kentucky, in August 1801 where over 3,000 came to Christ, doubling the attendance of the churches in the area.[13]

As the Second Great Awakening began to wane by the late 1840s, church attendance began to drop again. War was on the horizon, and the 1850s saw a period of increased violence and bloodshed. The Compromise of 1850 and the Kansas–Nebraska Act were the precursors of the great battle that awaited the nation a few years later. Fortunately, there were a group of churches praying in New York City that God would pour out His Holy Spirit again upon our country. Though there were a number of churches praying, the most famous story, which was discussed in Chapter 3, is the prayer meeting begun by Jeremiah Lanphier on September 23, 1857, at the Dutch Reformed Church on Fulton Street. By February 1858, every church and public hall in New York City was filled with people praying. By March 1858, a landslide of prayer began in every city, with people beginning to be converted at a rate of 10,000 people per week in a city with a population of 800,000. By May, it was estimated that over 50,000 people had been converted in New York City. By the end of 1858, J. Edwin Orr believes that about 1.4 million people joined the Church, raising the total church attendance from four million to five million people, or about thirty-five percent of the entire population.[14]

Fifty-six years later, the Great Welsh Revival would erupt in Wales in 1904 when a humble coal miner and Bible student, Evan Roberts, pleaded with the Lord to "bend me," and the Lord told him that he would have 100,000 souls. This would occur within the next five months. Roberts tried to return to his classes but was compelled to go back to his home church and speak to the young people. The pastor allowed him to speak after a Monday meeting, and seventeen people stayed. He told them to repent of any unconfessed sin, to put away any doubtful habit, to obey the Spirit promptly, and to confess Christ publicly. All seventeen responded. Roberts was invited to speak each day that week and into the following week. During the second week, the Holy Spirit was poured out upon the Church, and suddenly great crowds of people flocked to Loughor. Within three months, over 70,000 people were converted to Christ. Revival broke out across Wales, and within five months, there were over 100,000 people converted outside the Church and 150,000 converted within the Church.[15]

When news of the revival came to the USA, the Southern Baptist Magazine ran an article entitled "Will God Send Revival Here?". In the article, the author scolded the Baptist church for trying to manufacture a revival. "We are doing the inconsistent thing. We read the Welsh revival has no machinery, and yet we are trying to get our machinery going."[16] Fortunately, a small Welsh church was praying that God would do in their church what He was doing in their homeland of Wales, and in December 1904, revival broke out and 123 were converted.

In early 1905, the revival swept to Philadelphia, where the Methodists reported over 10,000 conversions, and Atlantic City, where virtually the entire city accepted Christ. In New York City, the Brooklyn Baptist Temple reported over 500 conversions, and Calvary Methodist Episcopal Church stated 364 people received Christ on the first Sunday in February 1905.[17] By mid-1906, there were reports of over one million people converted to Christ. On

April 14, 1906, the Apostolic Faith Mission on Azusa Street experienced a revival, and within their small, simple building, the congregation grew from 100 to 350, which became famously known as the "Azusa Street Revival." The revival was reignited and swept a second time back across the USA.[18]

These revivals greatly strengthened the churches across all denominations. This became a worldwide revival that not only swept through North America, but also Europe, Africa, Australia, and Asia. It is estimated that over five million people were converted in two years.[19] These revivals did not just bring new converts to the Churches and increase church enrollments but brought the power of the Holy Spirit and a renewed sense of purpose and conviction to the Churches. People were not only confessing sin and being converted but taking action. The Churches mobilized together to affect the social reforms of the day. Many of the laws passed in the early 20th century involving child labor, women's rights, and temperance were a direct result of this revival and the activity of Christians promoting these reforms in our country.

This phenomenon not only occurred in North America but in other parts of the world. As discussed in chapter 5, the Korean Revival had a dramatic impact on the country. It was reported that people would go to their neighbors confessing articles that they had stolen, bearing witness to the entire city of what Christ had done.

> *Repentance was by no means confined to confession and tears. Peace waited upon reparation, wherever reparation was possible. We had our hearts torn again and again during those days by the return of little articles and money that had*

> *been stolen from us during the years. It hurt so to see them grieve. All through the city men were going from house to house, confessing to individuals they had injured, returning stolen property and money, not only to Christians but to heathen as well, till the whole city was stirred. A Chinese merchant was astonished to have a Christian walk in and pay him a large sum of money that he had obtained unjustly years before.*[20]

Throughout our history, our great revivals greatly strengthened the churches in numerical growth but also in impacting our culture. A significant minority of the population were converted and became members of the church. Also, the churches united together and had one voice as they proclaimed the gospel and also addressed social issues in their day. The churches had a dramatic impact on the values of the culture and shifted our societal priorities because people's hearts had been transformed. Because of the changes that occurred within the souls of millions of individuals, the priorities of our society were changed.

Should this not be the goal for our churches today? We have plenty of constructs and programs to try to draw people to our church services, but what people are really looking for is the presence and power of God. People want the real experience of an encounter with their Creator not the poor attempt of a manufactured experience. They want an encounter with the One who knows and loves them. The challenge is we cannot manufacture that experience, but we can pray for it.

CHAPTER 7

WHAT MAKES A REVIVAL GREAT?

Perhaps the greatest barrier to revival on a large scale is the fact that we are too interested in a great display. We want an exhibition; God is looking for a man who will throw himself entirely on God. Whenever self-effort, self-glory, self-seeking, or self-promotion enters into the work of revival, then God leaves us to ourselves.

—Sadhu Sundar Singh

What If God Brings Revival?

THE HISTORIAN DR. PERRY Miller, who taught history at Harvard University and was not a Christian, referred to the Prayer Revival of 1857 as the premier event of the 19th century. This is amazing when you consider that the Civil War was occurring at the same time as this revival. I am sure many historians would not agree with this statement, but the point that Dr. Miller is making is that this Prayer Revival was a major event in our history. The same can definitely be said about the Second Great Awakening. Dr. Edward O'Donnell, who is a professor of history at the College of the Holy Cross, selected the Second Great Awakening as one of the major turning points in U.S. history.[1]

The revivals which occurred are major historical events that changed our society and reshaped the values we believe in. If these revivals do not occur, we are a different country, and we do not have the same values that we all espouse today. This is a historical fact. What is tragic is how few history classes acknowledge the great revivals. Even more disturbing is how few Christians are aware of these revivals and the impact they had on our history. If you are unaware of the revivals, then you have no motivation to pray that they will occur again. This is why educating our church on the revivals is paramount to creating a motivation for prayer that God will pour out His Spirit.

Every revival is unique, and probably historians and church theologians would differ on why one revival is considered "great" and not another. Revivals have occurred frequently throughout our past, and based on the definition that revival is transformation, every Christian has been revived in their soul. However, when the claim is made that there has not been a "great" revival in over 120 years, what is the reasoning? Why would the Jesus Movement in the 1970s not be considered a great revival, as it definitely had a clear impact on thousands of people? This is a fair question.

> **A "great revival" is one that involves the entire nation, including all ages and demographics.**

As you review all the past revivals, you will see that a "great revival" is one that involves the entire nation, including all ages and demographics. And though it began in the Churches, it swept through towns and cities so that everyone was aware of it and affected by it. It forced almost every person to make a decision on whether or not they would accept Christ as their Savior. It was not just the headline of the day, but it was the major event for several years. It not only significantly increased church attendance, but it impacted society. The culture shifted in terms of its beliefs and headed in a significantly different course. The nation was not the same after the revival dissipated.

In Western society, religion is viewed by society as a private matter. This is a direct effect of the Enlightenment, in which religion and science were delegated to different spheres of reality. Science became the guardian of truth, and religion became personal opinion. What you choose to believe is your choice, but please respect my position also. What I believe about religion is just as valid as what you believe since it is all subjective. This makes it very difficult to share the gospel since everyone's position has the same validity. This is why Christians are very reluctant to discuss their faith with anyone because it feels like you are intruding on a person's private life. Besides, who am I to tell someone what they believe is wrong? These feelings that we all share are the voices of our culture saying to mind your own business. And we only overcome it when we realize the lie that our society is shouting at us, which is that truth does not exist in religion.

Ironically, science does not hold truth as absolute either, as the theorems of science are always being questioned and re-evaluated. In our legal system, truth is based on "evidence beyond a reasonable doubt." So, when Jesus claims to be the way, the truth, and the life, do we have evidence beyond a reasonable doubt? The answer is yes, based on the historical evidence of the resurrection, the same as any other historical event where reasonable and verifiable witnesses recorded the event. A jury of nine can proclaim the truth in our court system, but the resurrection is supported by over 500 witnesses testifying to this truth. Does this matter to our society? The answer is no. Because our culture says facts do not exist in religion since it is only a personal opinion.

In a great revival, these categories of belief are challenged significantly. The revival has such an impact on the culture that people cannot pretend that it does not matter what they believe because it is all a matter of personal opinion. This can be attributed to the intense wave of the Holy Spirit that sweeps across the nation during a great revival. It is truly a tsunami that people cannot ignore. Since no one alive has experienced it, it is hard to picture what it is like. But when the wave hits a town, people across all demographics are suddenly swept up in its fury, and people who had no interest in church are suddenly convicted of their sin and are running to the church for spiritual counsel. It is commonplace to hear stories of people drinking in the bar or dancing or conducting business suddenly feeling convicted and leaving what they are doing and seeking counsel regarding their spiritual condition.

As stated in chapter 3, there were about 25,000 people present at the Cane Ridge Campfire revival in August 1801. This was a remarkable number when you consider that the largest town in Kentucky—Lexington—only numbered 1,797. When the wave of the Holy Spirit came through Kentucky, everyone was swept up in it. Robert Davidson reported the following: *"Businesses of all kinds were suspended; dwelling houses were deserted; whole neighborhoods emptied; bold hunters and sober matrons, young men, maidens, and little children flocked to the common center of attraction; every difficulty was surmounted, every risk ventured, to be present at the camp-meeting."*[2] Imagine if every person in your city was compelled to attend a revival meeting in your area.

Only one year prior, this area was filled with outlaws and fugitives who scoffed at both the law and the Church. Going to a revival meeting was the last thing on their minds. But when the power of the Holy Spirit came, they were overwhelmed. It was estimated about 3,000 people were saved during this event. Later, when George Baxter, President of Washington and Lee University in Virginia, traveled to Kentucky, he wrote, "I have never seen such a moral community in all my life, a religious awe seemed to pervade the entire country."[3] This was the same area where lawlessness was rampant only two years prior and was known as Rogue's Harbor because no one felt safe.

When the Welsh Revival came to the USA, there was not a town that escaped the sweeping blow of the Holy Spirit. The revival initiated in Pennsylvania and swept westward all the way to Seattle and Los Angeles, where every single town across the country reported thousands of conversions, all within a period of fifteen months.

- In Dixon, Illinois, the revival was described as a "cyclone" that hit the town.
- In Atlantic City, New Jersey, the entire town of 60,000 became Christians with less than a hundred people left unconverted.
- At Ashbury College, Kentucky, Henry Clay Morrison reported, "Salvation is the topic of conversation everywhere. On the streets, in the stores. Everyone is breathing a spiritual atmosphere."
- In Los Angeles, there were reported over 180,000 people attending prayer meetings.[4]

The *Christian Advocate* summed it up by saying, *"A great revival is sweeping the U.S. Its power is felt in every nook and corner of our broad land. The Holy Spirit is convincing the people of sin, of righteousness, and judgment to come. There is a manifest new degree of spiritual power in the churches."*[5] This is the essence of a "Great Revival." A revival where the movement of the Holy Spirit is so powerful that no one escapes the tsunami of powerful conviction as it sweeps across the country.

Every revival is a cause for celebration, but a great revival is a historical event. It is a unique phenomenon that occurs when God hears the pleas of His people over an extended period of time and pours out the vast riches of the Holy Spirit upon His people. People who were engulfed in sin, unbelief, and apathy are suddenly swept away by the joyous grace of God's Spirit, bringing conviction and victory over sin. As the revival sweeps through, the entire landscape is changed. And when every city and town is touched, the entire country is changed.

> **This is the essence of a "Great Revival." A revival where the movement of the Holy Spirit is so powerful that no one escapes the tsunami of powerful conviction as it sweeps across the country.**

A great revival is a unique experience that, if it occurred once in a person's life, would be remarkable and undoubtedly the event they would recall throughout their life. Unfortunately, none of us have witnessed this in our lifetime. It is not reasonable to expect a great revival to occur every year, but when it has not occurred in over a hundred years, there is a yearning for God to respond. This does not diminish the command for the church to continually be making disciples and evangelizing. But the influence of the church is limited in our culture, and the secular forces are marginalizing the impact of the church on society. Imagine the impact of a great revival on our country? Instead of seeking the lost, the lost are seeking the church.

As J. Edwin Orr stated, "In times of evangelism, the evangelist seeks the sinner. In times of revival, the sinner comes chasing after the Lord."[6] Suddenly, the gospel becomes a public matter, and becoming a believer is expected and celebrated by the community. The church is celebrated as a place of truth.

But in our modern age of technology and sophistication, is it reasonable to believe that God would pour out His Spirit in such a powerful wave that our entire country would turn to Him? Of course, it is not reasonable to believe this, because it is an issue of faith and not reason. Reason will take you directly to unbelief, which is the default for everyone who claims science and technology as their god. Faith focuses on the Almighty God, who is just as Sovereign as He was in 1795, 1856, and 1900 before each of our great revivals occurred.

The people who lived during these times could have made the same excuses regarding their modernism because it is a claim of pride that our society is now too sophisticated to need God to intervene, and thus, why should I pray? This is the heart of Deism that says God may have created the heaven and earth, but man is really in control of daily events. Or as Benjamin Franklin famously said, "God helps those who help themselves." Society has not changed, and neither has God. Every generation is just as prideful as previous generations in believing that they have it figured out.

Maybe revival sounds a little antiquated. Sure, God may have done something great two hundred years ago, but they needed His help back then! And if we focus on God bringing about revival, are we not forsaking the work of the Church? The Church has a lot of programs to do, and who has the time to pray for revival? They did not have all these programs, so it was easier for them. If our ancestors, who made the sacrifice to pray faithfully for revival, could visit us today, I think they would quickly shame us into understanding that prayer was just as sacrificial for them as it is for us today.

They would remind us that we have conveniences which save us huge amounts of time in doing daily tasks. We load a washing machine and a dishwasher, push a button, and forget about it. They spent hours doing tasks that now require a few minutes for us. If we spend thirty minutes traveling to church, that is a sacrifice, whereas most of them lived large distances from the church and traveled at a fraction of the speed we do today. No, it was not easy for them, and it is not easy for us. They did not pray because it made sense, or they had nothing else to do; they prayed because they were desperate and they had faith.

You can be desperate but still believe you can make it happen. By believing that, we are practicing Deists. We are holding a superficial belief in God while trusting in our reason and ability to get the work done. Deism was the prevalent belief in the 1780s until God showed His mighty power in the Second Great Awakening. Suddenly, the Church realized that only God could bring about transformation. Do we believe that the only answer for the Church is for God to pour out His Spirit, or do we act like it really is up to us to make it happen? The answer depends upon how desperate we are for God to work in a way that we know is impossible for man to accomplish. Then we are ready to commit to pray for God to do what only He can do. Do we really believe that God wants to do a mighty work and pour out His Spirit and bring another Great Revival to our churches, communities, and country?

CHAPTER 8

REVIVAL WILL CHANGE A NATION

> True spiritual revival is like a seething lava flow. It takes time to reach its destination, but when it does, its intense heat and formidable power alters everything in its path. It is the full measure of God's kingdom come to earth. No spectacle is more glorious—or terrifying.
>
> —George Otis

*T*HE HEART OF EVERY revival is change! First, change for the individual and then the Church, the community, and ultimately, the country. Not all revivals have succeeded in changing our country, but the great revivals have. Do we desire for our country to be changed by a great revival that would affect not only the Church but also all our social institutions and our belief system as a country? According to William McLoughlin, all past revivals resulted in a "period of fundamental social and intellectual reorientation of the American belief value system, behavior patterns, and institutional structure."[1] When a great revival sweeps through a country, it has a dramatic impact on that country and it changes the course of history.

> **God wants to bring revival to the Church so people have intimacy with Him and make disciples in the world.**

The irony is the changes that occur are usually not what people expect or even want because they cause significant upheaval in the status quo. Often, when people long for change, they are hoping for a return to old institutions from their past that bring back pleasurable memories. We all have a desire to revisit periods of our childhood that we perceive to be idyllic. But revivals never do that. They do not take us back to the past but move us into a new future reality that is different from what we have ever experienced before. God is not interested in taking us back in time to relive fond memories. God wants to bring revival to the

Church so people have intimacy with Him and make disciples in the world. As the Church accomplishes this mission, it has a profound impact on our society and belief system as a country. The structural reformations begin in the Church but slowly change society as belief systems are shifted, resulting in different values and institutional changes.

So how have the revivals brought change to our country? Many people believe that our American Revolution is the direct result of the First Great Awakening. Though historians would argue that the revolution was motivated by economic reasons, the deeper question is what enabled our forefathers to believe that they had the right to separate from Great Britain and declare independence? The First Great Awakening had a profound impact on how people perceived their identity. Before the Awakening, there was a strict adherence to and loyalty to the local church, and the church was an extension of the state. In the colonial period, there was a strong allegiance between the state and church. For example, Roger Williams planted the seed for the separation of church and state in the formation of Providence, Rhode Island; this concept was unknown in most of the colonies. Being a loyal royal subject of Great Britain meant weekly church attendance, church membership, adherence to a catechism, and participation in family prayers.[2]

In the 1740s, when Jonathan Edwards stressed the importance of a personal relationship with Jesus and millions of people were transformed by the Holy Spirit, they found that their relationship with God was more than just attending church and an intellectual belief in specific doctrines. Suddenly, their personal relationship with God superseded everything else.

As Isaac Backus proclaimed after his conversion, "The Lord God is a Sun...when any soul is brought to behold His Glories, the eternal rays of Light and Love shine down particularly upon him to remove his darkness."[3] Suddenly, people reoriented themselves to attend a local parish that fit more with their personal conviction rather than the social expectations put forth by the local government. Many people, similar to Isaac Backus, left the established church to start and attend Separatist churches. By 1755, there were 125 Separatist churches, and by 1776 there were an additional seventy Separatist Baptist churches in the country, all the result of the First Great Awakening.[4] People were declaring independence from the established church and the status quo. And if the colonists could form their own church, why not their own nation?

So, when the Declaration of Independence was signed in 1776, would it be accurate to say that America was founded as a Christian nation? According to a 2024 AP news poll, about sixty percent of Americans answer yes to this question.[5]

Based on the fact that the First Great Awakening had only occurred twenty-five years prior to America declaring its independence, this would seem like a reasonable assumption. But the motivation for the movement of independence and the religious life of the country at this time was very complex, as there were many interests and philosophies vying for the minds of Americans during this time.

There was a significant minority of Christians who had been affected by the First Great Awakening and had been transformed by the Holy Spirit and were living for Christ. But there was still a majority of people who chose to see religion as a positive thing since it provided good moral teachings and virtues for society but did not believe that a radical decision for Christ was necessary. In addition, there was a significant wave of Enlightenment philosophies coming to our nation from Europe, affecting both the intellectuals and young people. The Enlightenment was not just one particular teaching, but it did have a dramatic impact on how truth and religion were perceived.

The Enlightenment opened the door for the age of reason and the scientific method as the means to solve our problems. Why should we look to God to answer our prayers when God gave us reason and "common sense"? Suddenly, life became divided between the public and private spheres. Science became public and in the realm of reality and truth, whereas religion became private and in the realm of subjectivity and opinion. Truth was now only absolute in the area of science, but religion was subject to opinion and debate. In other words, the theories of science were truth, whereas the doctrines of the Bible could be debated. Thus, the theology of Deism, where God set the world in motion but is absent in the daily affairs of people, was becoming a predominant belief. It was a convenient meshing of philosophies to believe that there was still a God who created the universe, but that man was ultimately in control of his own destiny.

Yes, America was "religious," but the majority were not transformed by the gospel. Many held the outer wrappings of Christianity, but their core beliefs were Enlightenment thinking. But since many people created their own framework of beliefs, there was no consistency. Benjamin Franklin is a prime example of the confluence of various beliefs during this time and why trying to quantify whether or not America was a "Christian nation" during the American Revolution is so difficult and misleading.

Most people would consider Benjamin Franklin to be a Deist, and relatively speaking, this would be accurate. But there were many times in his life he did turn to God for personal pleas during difficult struggles, which a Deist would not do.[6]

On the other hand, he had serious reservations about orthodox Christianity, and he adamantly refused to accept Christ as his personal Savior even though Jonathan Edwards pleaded with him and he knew that Edwards was praying for him. He purposely chose to see the value of Christianity in regard to virtue and morals but could not accept the notion of an all-powerful God who was completely sovereign and in control of the affairs of mankind. Franklin even boasted regarding Whitefield, "He used indeed sometimes to pray for my conversion but never had the satisfaction of believing that his prayers were heard."[7]

Our founding fathers were on both ends of the spectrum: committed Christians and atheists. Charles Thomson, secretary to the Continental Congress, translated the entire Bible. Meanwhile, Thomas Paine was clearly an atheist who argued vehemently against Christianity. He wrote both the *Rights of Man* and the *Age of Reason*, which was even more popular. Both books sold over 1.5 million copies each and argued for human reason versus Christianity. In the book *Age of Reason*, Paine stated, "I have gone through the Bible as a man would go through the wood with an axe and felled trees. Here they lie and the priest may replant them, but they will never grow."[8]

As America gained her independence and entered the 1780s, the influence of Christianity waned significantly. Due to France's involvement in the war, America was enamored by French philosophy, but unfortunately, France had become an atheist nation.

The anti-Christian sentiment in France was so profound that the French crowned a prostitute "goddess of reason" in the Cathedral of Notre Dame. In addition, the French raised millions of dollars for the purpose of enlightening our younger generation with their new ideals. This generation became so fond of the French ideals and the age of reason that they held anti-Christian demonstrations on college campuses. At Harvard, the anti-Christian sentiment became so profuse that a poll found that there was only one believer in the entire student body. At Princeton, there was a total of two believers, and the students held a demonstration where they took all the Bibles out of the chapel and burned them in a public bonfire. The students at Williams College held a mock communion. The historian J. Edwin Orr stated, "There were so few Christians on campus by the 1790s that they met in secret cells and kept their minutes in code so that no one would know."[9]

The changes in our philosophical views and rejection of God also caused a significant decline in our moral behavior. Of the four million people in America, 300,000 were confirmed alcoholics and 15,000 per year were dying because of drunkenness. Benjamin Franklin even published over 200 terms for drunkenness in his newspaper *The Pennsylvania Gazette*.[10]

Profanity was commonplace, and many campuses had filthy speech clubs. Prostitution was legal, and sexually transmitted diseases were commonplace. Women were afraid of assault and would not go out at night. It was even worse in our Western frontier of Kentucky and Tennessee. If you committed a murder on the East Coast, you would just flee across the Appalachian Mountains. In Kentucky, there was no law enforcement and there was not one court of justice in over five years. Logan County in Kentucky was nicknamed "Satan's Stronghold" because of lawlessness, gambling, drunkenness, and immorality. The people tried to form a vigilante regiment against the outlaws and lost.[11]

When the Second Great Awakening occurred, the country was suddenly awakened to the false philosophies it had chosen to believe. **The pouring out of the Holy Spirit awoke the consciousness of the nation to recognize the active role that God plays in the personal affairs of men.** Suddenly, Deism, in which God is remote from the personal affairs of men and women, was no longer a reasonable teaching to believe. The superficial notion that the role of the church in society was solely for the virtue of morals and good behavior was seen as superficial.

As people came to Christ in large numbers and the Holy Spirit transformed large segments of the population, people attended church because they recognized that they are the body of Christ. In other words, the notion that the purpose of religion was solely to provide society a moral compass was no longer accepted. As people were convicted by the Holy Spirit, it also changed the behavior and values of the country. When contemporary Americans believe that the United States was founded as a Christian nation, as stated by the 2024 AP poll, their perception of America is based on the values of the country after the Second Great Awakening and not in 1776. The values of America radically shifted in the early 1800s, causing a rebirth of the population during this time.

The Second Great Awakening had a profound impact on the behavior and values of our nation. It caused the nation to turn 180 degrees to what was acceptable and true. The most dramatic change occurred in the Western frontier, where the entire culture shifted from total lawlessness to godliness. The incredible transformation to the entire area was summed up by George Baxter, President of Washington and Jefferson University, when he traveled to Kentucky in the fall of 1801.

> *"The power with which this revival has spread, and its influence in moralizing the people, are difficult for you to conceive of, and more difficult for me to describe...I found Kentucky the most moral place I had ever been in; a profane expression was hardly heard; a religious awe seemed to pervade the country;...I think the revival in Kentucky among the most extraordinary that have ever visited the Church of Christ and all things considered, a peculiarly adopted to the circumstances of that country where infidelity was triumphant and religion at the point of expiring. Something of an extraordinary nature seemed to arrest the attention of a giddy people, who were ready to conclude that Christianity was a fable."*[12]

This was the same area where a few years prior, vigilantes ruled, and any kind of law and order was completely absent. As a testimony to the philosophical shift in our nation, in the next sixty years, there were 160 colleges founded in America, mostly in the Midwest, and 144 of them were Christian colleges. Now, instead of learning enlightenment philosophies, our young people were being educated on Christian principles. This had a profound influence on our culture as our nation expanded westward. Instead of extending our territorial borders as a godless nation with no law, we expanded as a Christian nation upholding Biblical principles for society and law.

The Second Great Awakening initiated the era of modern-day missions, shifting Christianity from being solely a Western religion to a world religion. According to the historian Stephen Neill, "In 1800 it was still by no means certain that Christianity would be successful in turning itself into a universal religion."[13] The Second Great Awakening and the Revival of 1858 would dramatically change that.

In America, the light of missionary service was ignited by a group of students at Williams College who, one day, were caught in a thunderstorm while praying and sought cover in a haystack. While praying, they pledged themselves to missionary service, and this became known as the "haystack prayer meeting." They would form the American Board of Commissioners for Foreign Missions, who would send Adoniram Judson, the first American missionary to travel abroad. In 1812, he set sail for Burma, where he would spend nearly forty years translating the Bible into Burmese and establishing a Christian community, which still thrives today. The same board would also send missionaries to the West Coast ahead of settlers. Most notable were Marcus and Narcissa Whitman, who in 1836 were among the first Americans to travel all the way to the Oregon Territory to evangelize the Indians. In addition, the Baptist Missionary Society, the Church Missionary Society, and the London Missionary Society started sending out missionaries, creating the modern-day missionary movement.[14]

One of the most significant developments was the igniting of the abolitionist movement in the USA. Though abolition was known in the late 1700s, primarily with the Quakers, the issue of slavery as a national issue was ignored until the Second Great Awakening occurred. In 1808, America ended the importation of slaves from Africa and the West Indies. In 1833, the American Anti-Slavery Society was formed, publishing many pamphlets regarding the cruelty of slavery and the biblical argument against slavery. No longer was slavery being ignored or justified, but it was now being perceived as a clear injustice to mankind and a curse that must be eradicated.

The Second Great Awakening also affected the social issues of the day. In 1837, George Williams was converted, and being influenced by the lectures of Charles Finney on Revivals of Religion and Professing Christians, he founded the Draper's Evangelical Association which was later renamed the Young Men's Christian Association (YMCA). This organization focused on the deplorable working conditions in the cities and was very zealous in sharing the gospel to the masses.[15]

History does repeat itself, and the moral climate in our nation has fluctuated like a thermometer through the seasons of the year. Though long-held principles changed suddenly in the early 1800s, the conflict of slavery brought increased violence back to our nation in the 1850s. America was a divided nation regarding the slavery issue. In 1852, Harriet Beecher Stowe wrote *Uncle Tom's Cabin*, which revealed the cruelties of slavery and exposed the myths perpetuated by the South regarding the treatment of slaves by their masters. She claimed that God had given her visions that she wrote down. The book sold 300,000 copies in the first year and created over two million abolitionists overnight. When Abraham Lincoln met Harriet Beecher Stowe, he said, "Here is the little lady who caused the great war."

In 1854, the Kansas–Nebraska Act was passed, leading to "Bleeding Kansas," and thousands of armed Southerners crossed over from Missouri and kept people from the ballot box. About 150 were killed in the violence. Then, in 1856, Senator Charles Sumner of Massachusetts gave a blistering speech against slavery, and three days later, in the Senate chambers, Congressman Preston Brooks from South Carolina physically caned him until the cane was in splinters. The *Richmond Enquirer* wrote, "We consider the act good in conception, better in execution, and best of all in consequences. These vulgar abolitionists in the Senate must be lashed into submission." Even more shocking, the people of South Carolina sent Preston Brooks dozens of new canes to replace the one he splintered over Charles Sumner's head. Violence was increasing, and again church attendance was decreasing.[16]

But when the revival of 1857 occurred, there was suddenly a reawakening of the soul of America. Unlike the prior revival, this revival had no clear leader and was marked by organized prayer across the nation. By this time, it was clear that America was a deeply divided nation headed towards a bitter Civil War. Thankfully, this revival touched the souls of countless men and women, many of whom would fight and be killed in the war. There were about 620,000 deaths (more recent research has the total number at 750,000), which was about two percent of the entire population. But due to the Revival of 1857, it is estimated that over 150,000 Confederate soldiers were converted in the Northern Virginia army. As one pastor stated in 1865 regarding the impact of the revival of 1857, "The Lord was merciful in gathering His elect before the great war would sweep so many into eternity."[17]

The Revival of 1857 formed several new mission agencies with the commitment to reach every country in the world. In one of D.L. Moody's evangelistic campaigns, C.T. Studd, was converted, which shocked many people because of the fame of his family and great wealth. A few years later, C.T. Studd, along with six other students from Cambridge University, formed the Student Volunteer Movement committed to foreign missions and went to China. This movement became responsible for sending out 20,500 students, mostly to China and India. They were known for the intensity of their faith and willingness to adapt to the culture. It is estimated by the early 20th century that half of all Protestant missionaries were sent out by the Student Volunteer Movement. In addition, a number of faith mission societies were created, including the Christian and Missionary Alliance (1887), the Evangelical Alliance Mission (1890), the Sudan Interior Mission (1893), and the African Inland Mission (1895).[18]

Other mission initiatives were also in process. In 1858, Albert Simpson of Western Ontario was converted, and he later became the founder of the Christian and Missionary Alliance. In 1884, this organization sent five young men to Congo, Africa, beginning the process of opening up this continent. In 1898, the Sudan Interior Mission was formed by Rowland Bingham, and this mission was successful in penetrating Western Africa.[19]

In 1988, I spent the summer in the Republic of Congo. It has one of the highest Christian populations in the world. While I was there, the Christian and Missionary Alliance (CMA) had just celebrated its 100th anniversary of sending its first missionaries. But most of the missionaries who first went to Congo and the rest of Africa never returned due to tropical diseases. They said goodbye to their families and realized that the odds of coming home were remote. That is why they often left packing their belongings in a casket, which they would eventually be buried in.

During that summer, I was in the middle of the jungle when I woke up early one morning and went out to pray. I realized that I was looking at the gravestones of some of the earliest missionaries that the CMA had sent out, missionaries who literally gave their lives for sharing the gospel and starting the church in Congo, who would never return to loved ones in America. It is reported that for many years after the founding of the CMA, the number of missionary graves greatly outnumbered the living missionaries.[20] Again, I am not sure that the people who prayed in 1857 realized that a revival would occur in which we would send out thousands from our country who would be willing to die for the sake of Christ.

The Great Welsh revival came to the USA in 1904 and also became known in 1906 as the Asuza Street revival. It had a dramatic influence on church attendance as it is estimated that over one million people were converted and joined the church between 1904–1906.[21] This revival also ignited the modern day Pentecostal movement in the USA with a renewed emphasis on gifts of the Spirit and the infilling of the Holy Spirit in a person's life.

This revival prompted many social reforms to occur in our country. There were many injustices such as child labor, terrible working conditions, and poor sanitation along with heavy drinking, growing tobacco use, and prostitution. This revival occurred at the beginning of Billy Sunday's urban revivalist campaigns, and he had a dramatic influence on not only seeing millions of people being saved, but he also addressed the major social ills during this time. After preaching in Burlington, Iowa, the headline read, "Burlington is Dry: Billy Sunday has Made a Graveyard of Once Fast Town." The notion of temperance and controlling the consumption of alcohol had been actively occurring since 1860, but after this revival, it became a national issue. By 1916, twenty-three states passed laws banning the sale of alcohol leading to National Prohibition in 1920.[22]

The Great Revivals reshaped our nation and changed history. The 1800s would have been completely different without the Second Great Awakening and the Prayer Revival of 1857. The Second Great Awakening completely reversed the growing immorality of the nation and brought many reforms to our country. This revival ushered in the "Victorian Era" with the social and political reforms that we often associate with the 19th century. It also initiated the modern-day missionary movement, changed the philosophy and education in all our colleges, created many Christian societies, and awakened abolition. The Prayer Revival of 1857 ignited the holiness movement and initiated many of the mission societies that we know today. The thousands of missionaries who have been sent out around the world are a direct result of this revival. The Welsh Revival which became the Azusa Street revival in the USA ignited the modern day Pentecostal movement and also introduced many social reforms in our country.

Our nation was dramatically impacted by these revivals and the values in our society were realigned reflecting Biblical beliefs that gave glory to God. Before each of these revivals, society was trending away from God and there was a feeling of despair amongst the Christians that the situation was hopeless. But in the moment of desperation, they chose to resort to their greatest weapon which was prayer. They could have chosen to focus on a political crusade believing that they would bring change through the ballot box by electing the correct politicians. However, they understood real change would only occur through the power of God and the pouring out of the Holy Spirit. I suspect few Christians really believed that the nation could be changed when they started praying, but they chose prayer as the remedy for the country and God responded. They were able to witness the greatest transformation of our country through these great revivals. What they probably believed was impossible when they decided to pray, they witnessed the power of God as He brought complete transformation to our country. There is always a temptation to bring about change from the outside; when we believe we can change the mind of the person, their heart will follow, but this only creates enemies. Real change in both the person and the culture occurs from the inside out when the heart is transformed by the Holy Spirit bringing change to the person and that ultimately brings change to the culture. Only the Holy Spirit can transform the soul, and this is why we must pray for God to work. We can see the same again if we follow their path and commit to pray for God's Spirit to be poured out on our country again.

CHAPTER 9

WHAT IF... REVIVAL?

They tell me a revival is only temporary; so is a bath, but it does you good.

—Billy Sunday

HER SENIOR YEAR IN high school, my daughter was on a 4x800 track team that won the Ohio state championship. It was a thrilling day, as much for me as for her, as we all entered Jesse Owens Stadium in Columbus, Ohio, with the 10,000 fans screaming at each event. But my daughter was not alone; she was part of a team of four girls. For the team to win, each had to do their part. Each one had to have their best time ever. They had already won their district and regional meets, so winning the state championship was a possibility, but not a given. The first girl did great and was slightly ahead as she handed the baton off to the second girl. The second girl also did her job, staying even with the competitor, and my daughter received the baton one step ahead of the second-place school. When my daughter got the baton, the girl she was even with suddenly slowed down, and my daughter was confused. My daughter knew this girl was fast and had beaten her in previous meets. Not wanting to go out too fast, my daughter slowed down also, but suddenly a third girl passed them both. My daughter had a quick decision to make. Does she stay with the girl who is going slow or accelerate to keep up with the girl that just passed her? She accelerated and stayed with her for the remaining 700 meters. She handed off the baton about four meters behind the girl who passed her. This was a crucial decision in the race.

Our generation currently has the baton. What are we going to do with the baton as we run the race for our Lord? Yes, we are called to be sharing the gospel and to be making disciples. But without a great movement of the Holy Spirit, we will not make a great impact on our society and see millions saved. We are not called to do this because we want a more comfortable country to live in. We are called because we want Jesus Christ honored as the

King of Kings and Lord of Lords. We want our churches to be holy, where people repent of their sins and the Holy Spirit draws thousands in each city to Himself. This is what God has done in the past. Why can we not believe He can do it again?

As we look back over the past three centuries in our history, we can see the church's influence rise and fall in the culture. The influence is directly related to the percentage of people who were being saved in all the churches in America. The great revivals had the most significant impact on salvations, church attendance, and societal changes in our culture during that time. The revivals impacted each generation profoundly and changed the course of history as the country turned the rudder and headed in a different direction. This all occurred because that generation of people was desperate enough to commit to pray for revival until God poured out His Spirit on the church. They all took the step of faith, believing that God would hear their prayers and that if they continued to pray, He would do a mighty work in His Spirit. We can credit each generation for their sacrificial prayers; they trusted the Lord and made faithful praying a priority.

Each generation is faced with the question, "Do I believe that God will answer the cries of His people if we unite faithfully in prayer and persevere until His Spirit comes?" Prayer is not easy and requires believing that God is faithful. What will our generation believe? The generations who answered "Yes" to this question were motivated by desperation. They saw the church failing to have an influence in their society. As a matter of fact, many thought the church was dead and Christianity would disappear. In their despair, they cried out to God to revive their church. But they did not just cry out for just one day, one month, or one year, but many years. Are we up to that challenge? Or will we hand the baton to the next generation, saying it was not that important to us? Will we just tolerate mediocrity and live peacefully with the social tensions of the day that wage war against the church? It is no big deal. If that is our answer, then we are not desperate enough. Or we just don't believe that God really will send an outpouring of His Spirit. However, in making that conclusion, we are saying that the stories of the Great Revivals of the past are exaggerated, or for some bizarre reason, we just don't believe that God would do it again, regardless of whether we pray or not.

> **Each generation is faced with the question, "Do I believe that God will answer the cries of His people if we unite faithfully in prayer and persevere until His Spirit comes?"**

I refuse to accept that conclusion. When I look back on our history and see the incredible things that God has done, I am inspired to believe that God will do it again if His church prays fervently until revival comes. But if we do not pray, then we can guarantee that a revival will not occur. All revivals occurred as a result of prayer, and no revival ever happened without prayer. The Bible and history tell us that God will move in power amongst His people when His church prays.

We all make choices in our lives about what we prioritize. It is incredibly sad that corporate prayer is a low priority in most churches. I understand that our culture contains many distractions that keep us from praying. But the truth is, we all choose what our priorities will be, and we typically base that on what will give us the most satisfaction. The challenge is that prayer rarely brings immediate gratification. God works on His timetable, and the answers might occur long after the prayer. It often requires consistent praying for God to answer. This is not encouraging, so we do not prioritize it. As a result, the Church remains powerless and has minimal impact on the culture around it.

Do you believe that if the Church prays fervently and continuously, God will eventually send a great revival that will impact the entire landscape of our country? It is easy to answer yes to this question but then not take any action. But how can we answer yes and then not care? If God sends an outpouring of His Spirit and millions are saved, is that not worth a great sacrifice on our part? Or are we so self-consumed with our priorities that focusing on prayer will never rise to be the priority it deserves? We can spend hours doing very little in our lives. We can even spend hours planning church events that result in very little because it is not a priority for God. Prayer is a priority for God. Corporate prayer from His Body united together is a top priority for God. When the Church unites together to pray and does so with a determination that pounds on the gates of heaven, then God will absolutely answer.

I am so grateful for the generations before me who believed this truth. They refused to believe the lie that prayer does not matter or that doing practical things is more important. Every generation decides its priorities and has the same excuses to be distracted or not. Fortunately, we have a few generations in our history who chose the hard road. They chose to pray continuously and refused to give up even when heaven was silent for years. They persisted because they believed that their prayers would be heard. God answered with a mighty and powerful outpouring of His Spirit that shocked the nation and turned it upside down. No program or methodology in the Church can duplicate a revival, not even close. When God's Spirit moves throughout the land, people are confronted with their sin, multitudes are saved, and society is changed.

Are we going to be the generation who will believe and take action in prayer? It begins one person at a time, like Jeremiah Lanphier in 1857, and one church at a time, and one city at a time until it spreads from county to county and state to state and across the country. Yes, it can happen again—if we choose to believe that this is a priority in our lives and in the life of our church and country.

Praying for revival is not a great sacrifice. When the people signed the North Carolina Covenant, they were committing to pray and fast the third Saturday of each month, and they also agreed to pray for Pastor James McGready for thirty minutes on Saturday evening and at sunrise on Sunday morning. In other words, they were committing to pray one hour every weekend and during one Saturday. It was not rearranging their entire lives, but it was a very serious commitment that did involve sacrifice. They prayed for three years with no results. They signed a covenant that they would pray until God sent revival or they died. That is the key. Not the frequency, but the commitment that the pouring out of God's Spirit on Logan County, Kentucky was so important that they would continue to pray until it happened or they died. What would happen in our country if we made the same commitment and lived up to it? In our hearts, we know the answer, but it is the commitment that scares us because it involves sacrifice.

For those people who made the commitment and prayed for three years, when they heard the news of the thousands of people coming to Christ in the summer of 1800, did they feel like they had wasted their time? It is not an exaggeration to say that the people who signed the North Carolina Covenant and sacrificed for three years in prayer changed the course of history in America. After the Louisiana Purchase, our country was moving west, eventually all the way to the Pacific Ocean. After the Second Great Awakening, the Western states of Ohio, Kentucky, and Tennessee became godly places where morality and Christian virtues were paramount.

As the pioneers moved west, they took Christianity and these values with them. Imagine if this revival did not occur and the predominant morality was represented by the outlaws of Logan County, Kentucky, as we pushed west. We would have formed a different country. Of course, it is hard to envision this, but it is the truth. What we perceive to be the Christian values that we often cherish are a result of these revivals that transformed thousands of people and radically changed the landscape of our country.

When that generation was handed the baton, they ran the race with perseverance, keeping their eyes fixed on Jesus, and they prayed into the will of God until He sent His Holy Spirit. It is now our turn. We have the baton. What are we going to do with it? Are we going to run with it, or at least walk with it, or just throw it away? The prior generation is now the "great cloud of witnesses" (Hebrews 12:1) who are looking at what we will do. Figuratively, they are cheering us on to be faithful. The question is if we will run with the baton and fix our eyes on the finish line. The writer of Hebrews urges us to run the race and to not allow sin to take us out of the race. This means we must decide if the prize at the finish line is worth the cost of the sacrifice of running the race. The signers of the North Carolina Covenant tell us, "Yes!"

The sacrifice does not involve rearranging your entire life, but it does mean making space in your life for prayer. Without corporate prayer, there is no revival. Are you in? Do you believe that prayer will make a difference? We all wish it would happen immediately, but it might not. We must be sober and understand that the race is a marathon and not a sprint.

The longest running race in the world is the Self-Transcendence 3100 Mile Race held annually in Queens, New York City. The race lasts for about fifty-two days, and the runners run around a single block a total of 5,649 times, averaging over sixty miles a day. This means they see the same sights 5,649 times as they run in a big circle until they finally reach the finish line. In the description of the race, the organizers state that the race is a test of "monotony" as you run around the same block.

If people can choose to sign up for such a race, can you sign up for a race that has real eternal consequences? It is easy to answer yes to the challenge until you run 108 times around the same block on Day 1 and you realize that you still have fifty-one days left. Suddenly, the scope of the challenge intensifies and there a million reasons to stop running. Unfortunately, there is no medal for the people who stop and there is no revival for those who no longer pray. There have been many people who start with great intentions but are quickly discouraged and lose interest.

Why did previous generations not lose interest but continue to pray for several years? First, there probably were many people who did quit, but they are forgotten in history. Second, I believe the fact that many people committed to pray together across multiple denominations encouraged perseverance. If they continued to pray, then I could also. Third, the fact that some people actually signed a covenant to pray "until God sent revival or they died" encouraged them to continue praying. Though there was nothing legally binding, they made a commitment to a friend who had made the sacrifice to travel to the remote parts of the frontier where lawlessness reigned, believing that God would do the impossible. With this knowledge, they had serious motivation not to disappoint their friend.

Unfortunately, in my experience, people get excited to pray for revival and will initially commit to praying. And even though they are warned that this is a long-term commitment when they start, they quickly lose interest and find other things that will bring a quicker reward for their effort. Praying for revival is like making microwave popcorn. You cannot speed up the process. You must patiently wait for the entire time, and it suddenly happens, but praying for revival is more challenging because we don't know how long we must wait.

In chapter 4, I mentioned how prayer can be waiting for the microwave popcorn to pop. The microwave popcorn instructions tell us to cook it for 2.5 minutes, so we can be confident at two minutes we are almost there and only need to wait thirty more seconds. With revival, God does not tell us how long we must pray. Are we halfway there or ninety percent or less? Regardless, it should not matter. We are not making popcorn but seeking salvation for thousands of people. Is that not worth the sacrifice? The people who signed the North Carolina Covenant said yes, and they committed to prayer until God brought revival, or they died. Would they have continued for twenty years? We do not know.

But they did pray for three years with no results. I believe that God will test our determination and faith, and we do not know how long that will be. We do not know the length of the course, but we know the prize that awaits us.

What if God does not bring revival? This is a fair question, but history tells us that if we faithfully pray as the Church corporately, revival will come. God has promised that He will pour out His Spirit on a praying church, but we just do not know the exact timetable. This is an issue of faith and perseverance. Yes, it is very hard to continue to pray for two years every week with no results. Friend, there are results in the heavenly realm, we just don't see them. In chapter 10 of the Book of Daniel, Daniel was praying and fasting for three weeks before he was visited by an angel to tell him what was written in the book of truth. The angel explained that on the first day that Daniel began praying, he was heard and the angel responded but was held back by the prince of the Persian kingdom for twenty-one days until Michael came to help the angel (v. 12–13).

The kernels are not the same after two minutes in the microwave, but they are not popcorn either. After two minutes, the water in the kernels has turned into steam, but the outside is not changed. But once the pressure inside reaches 135 psi and the temperature is 356°F, the kernel explodes and we have popcorn. We are patient because we know that the kernels will pop. We are 100 percent confident. We need that same confidence when we pray for revival.

Can we trust the promises of God the same as we trust the instructions on the back of a microwave popcorn package? Why do we trust those instructions? If we had never seen popcorn before, would we believe them? Maybe, but it would be more difficult.

Still, the fact that we all have seen popcorn made thousands of times gives us total confidence it will occur. Similarly, we can look back into history and acknowledge that God will do as He has promised because He has many times before. It is not a vain hope, but one that has been proven. The challenge is no one is alive now to give personal testimony, but the accounts are real. We believe in the resurrection because of the many firsthand recorded accounts. The same is true for revival. We have thousands of eyewitness accounts of what God accomplished after His church prayed. We know that these people were not exaggerating because they were corroborated by many others.

At the beginning of her track season, there was no indication that my daughter's team would win the state championship in Ohio. But when my daughter handed the baton to our very talented fourth girl, our anchor, there was little doubt. She shot out of the box, passing her competitor within the first thirty meters and never looked back. I will never forget the memory of seeing her come down the final stretch leading by fifteen meters, knowing that our team was going to be the state champions for the 4x800 event in Ohio. Later, her coach said to me that my daughter's decision to stay with the girl who passed her was the most crucial decision of the race. Ironically, the week before, my daughter had been voted the "unsung hero" by the team. She was rarely in the paper and not heavily recruited. However, her part on the team was crucial, and without her, the team does not win.

Most of us are "unsung heroes" in the Kingdom of God, but we now have the baton, and it is our turn to run. Are we going to give it our all and be faithful to the call of God on our lives? Or will we just go with the culture and not be concerned about the spiritual climate of the millions of people around us? You can do your role by organizing people to pray for revival in your church. Share the stories of what God has done in our past and challenge people to believe for the future. Each generation must make this choice to run with perseverance and to keep their eyes on Jesus. When my daughter stood on the platform with her team getting the medal for first place, she had no regrets about the many hours of running and training when no one was around. Likewise, when God brings revival and transforms the churches, we will not regret the decision we made to commit to pray for revival, believing that God would hear and answer our prayers. We have the baton, so let's run with it!

CONCLUSION

HOW HARD WOULD IT be to pray twice a month for revival? Imagine if hundreds of churches and thousands of Christians in our country made praying for revival a priority. Would these prayers make a difference in the life of your church, in your community, and in our country? This is the question of faith for every believer. The Bible and history say yes, but what do you say? How long are you willing to pray for revival? One month or two? Or could you make a commitment for one year or two? Praying a total of twenty-four times in a year, every other week, with other Christians. Though this does not sound too arduous, we know that it does involve real sacrifice. What sacrifice is worth experiencing a major revival in our country again?

I do not believe that prayer has ever been easy for any generation, but I do think that it is more difficult now than ever before due to the myriad of choices available to distract our time, or should I say, waste our time. Recreation and enjoyment will always be easier choices than prayer. We have more opportunities for recreation than ever before. The choices are endless and quickly accessible, usually an iPhone away. The invention of social media and the smartphone have made it unbelievably simple to escape into a different reality and waste large chunks of time that could be used for more productive ventures. We all know that the reason we pray little is not because we have so little time, but because we waste our time doing so little.

So, how can we make better choices to take some of these unproductive chunks of time and make them profitable by seeking intimacy with the Lord and spending time in prayer with each other? We need to encourage each other with the wonderful stories of how God has answered prayer in our past. I am amazed at how little is known about the great revivals in our history and the mighty work of God that was accomplished. Our nation has been shaped by these revivals.

When I tell the stories, people are amazed at what God did. But they are even more surprised to learn how desperate the church was before the revivals and how people were motivated to pray because they needed God to do a mighty work. Though these things occurred many years ago, they are part of our past and need to be heard. They should be told to our children as part of their history lessons and illustrations in our Bible lessons. They need to be preached on Sundays as examples of the wonderful way God has intervened. When people hear the details of how God moved and the mighty things He did to change our country virtually overnight, they are amazed and motivated to pray. They understand that there is no substitute for the power of the Holy Spirit working in the Church, calling people to repentance and prayer.

We need to make prayer a priority in the Church. The most powerful tool the Church has is to pray in faith for a movement of God. It cannot be an afterthought or how meetings are opened or closed but the lifeblood of the Church. It has to be a main dish served on a regular basis, not just the appetizer or dessert. This is not to discourage our programs or discipleship, which are essential, but without prayer, you have no gas for the engine.

Is your church willing to commit to pray twice a month for revival for your city and country? I would welcome the opportunity to come to your church and share the wonderful stories of revival regarding what God has done in our past and how it shaped who we are today and what we believe. I am praying for thousands of churches across all denominations to join in a prayer movement for revival. Please contact me at www.realrevival.com to discover how your church can actively participate.

LETTER TO PASTORS

Dear Pastor,

Thank you for taking the time to read my book on the great revivals in our history and the impact they had on our churches, communities, and country. I wrote this book to educate people on our history, as I have learned that very few understand the impact the revivals had on the growth of the church in our country. It is my hope that everyone will be motivated to pray for revival. I believe that in order for a great revival to occur again in our country, your commitment to encourage and support a prayer movement in your church is vital. Without your engagement, it will not happen. Every great revival occurred because of prayer, and the prayer occurred because the pastors took the lead.

Similar to past revivals, a movement of prayer across many denominations can only come with the support of the pastors who believe that this is the will of God, and revival is the answer for our churches, communities, and country. So please pray about how God would have you respond to His plea for His people to repent and pray in order for Him to heal our land.

I do believe it is God's will for every church to be praying for their church, community, and country. God wants all people to be transformed, and that will only occur through the Holy Spirit. Every generation of pastors had to decide how they would respond to the political and social forces that are hostile to the church. What we are experiencing today is not new, just different. Every pastor before our nation was born was tempted to succumb to the current cultural trends and not create waves that would make enemies of the church.

In Chapter 2, I discussed how Isaac Backus no longer felt comfortable in his parish church because his pastor did not want to exclude anyone who was not clearly converted and transformed from membership in the church. So, Backus and others formed Separatist churches that upset the status quo. This occurred in 1741, so the tension to please the masses in our society versus upholding the truth of the gospel and the transforming power of the Holy Spirit has been present for a long time.

Isaac Backus learned from this experience, so fifty-three years later in 1794, when society was again seeking to crush the church, he did not succumb and seek parity with culture but instead organized many pastors and churches to begin praying for revival. His history and vision told him that God was greater than the cultural trends and that God would change both the church and the country if His people prayed in faith.

Likewise, when James McGready goes to the most evil county in our nation known as Rogue's Harbor, he does not go with the strategy to elect political leaders or judges who will be more accommodating to the church. Before he leaves, he organizes over 200 people to sign the North Carolina Covenant and they commit to pray three times a month: the third Saturday of each month and for thirty minutes on Saturday evening and thirty minutes on Sunday morning. This was clearly a sacrifice, but it was reasonable and doable. The key is they committed to pray until either revival came or they died. For me, this is the missing link. We commit to pray, but only for short periods of time. They prayed for three years with no results before revival occurred. This is where your support and vision is so important. We must encourage our people that perseverant prayer will pay rich dividends in impacting our churches, communities, and country. But we need to believe it and run the race with perseverance.

My prayer is that a large network of churches will say "yes" to this challenge and commit to pray with perseverance. I believe hearing the stories from our past can help motivate people, but the truth is it will only occur with your commitment. You need to be "all in" in believing that God wants to and will heal our land if we persevere in prayer. I will do everything I can to assist you in this endeavor.

As a pastor, I do understand the challenge you face in getting people motivated to pray together. But I do believe that when people understand the possibilities of God impacting our communities and country with the power of the Holy Spirit, some will respond. If we can get a few from every church to respond, God will hear our prayers. I do not know how many people were praying in every church before the Second Great Awakening, but it was not everyone. But those who did pray committed to pray at sunset on Saturday night and sunrise on Sunday morning for thirty minutes. We need to educate our people on the promises of God and what God did and trust Him to raise the people to pray for the next revival. Would it be possible to get a commitment from a group of people in your church to pray for the revival of your community once a week for thirty minutes? It could be a small group formed in the church for this purpose or individuals who sign up because they are compelled by the Holy Spirit to pray for another revival.

I would love the opportunity to come to your church to share the incredible stories of our past and the amazing miracles that God performed when revival came. The stories will encourage your church to pray, but the commitment must come from you. In my experience, people hear the stories and are very enthused about praying initially, but that excitement quickly wanes as nothing happens. Again, our forefathers prayed for three years before revival occurred. And it can be longer, but I believe that if many churches are praying, God will respond in mighty power to the pleas of His people.

If you are interested in learning more about how you can participate, please go to www.realrevival.com. On this website, there is a commitment form to complete if your church is willing to join a network of churches to pray for revival, along with other helpful tools about how to organize a prayer movement in your church. When you complete this form, I will be in contact with you and will send you updates on what God is doing around the world in terms of revivals, with the hope that your church will continue to be inspired to pray. My vision is that future generations will look back at this time and be grateful that we were willing to make the sacrifice to pray for revival, just as we look back to our predecessors and thank them for their commitment and sacrifice. Thank you for taking the time to read this book, and I pray that you are inspired to take the steps to initiate the next Great Revival in our country.

ENDNOTES

CHAPTER 2:
1. William G. McLoughlin, *Revivals, Awakenings, and Reform* (Chicago: University of Chicago Press, 1978), 64.
2. Ibid., 65.
3. Ibid., 66.
4. Justin Taylor, "Billy Graham's Madison Square Garden Campaign, 60 Years Later," *The Gospel Coalition*, June 22, 2017, https://www.thegospelcoalition.org/blogs/evangelical-history/billy-grahams-madison-square-garden-campaign-60-years-later.

CHAPTER 3:
1. Glenda Orme Clark, *A Table in the Frontier: Pioneers, Protestants and the Presence of God* (2016), 116.
2. J. Edwin Orr, *The History of Revival and Spiritual Awakenings* (Van Nuys, CA: Church on the Way, 1981), "The Awakening of 1792 Onward."

3. *A Sermon on the Present Revival of Religion, Preached at the Opening of the Kentucky Synod* (Lexington, KY, 1803).
4. J. Edwin Orr, *The Light of the Nations* (Eugene, OR: Wipf & Stock, 2006), 103.
5. Ibid., 104.
6. Ibid., 109.
7. Ibid., 122.
8. Orr, *The History of Revival and Spiritual Awakenings*, "The Awakening of 1792 Onward."
9. Orr, *The History of Revival and Spiritual Awakenings*, "The Awakening of 1904 in Wales."

CHAPTER 4:

1. "We Asked 7,454 Christians How Often They Pray — And the Results Were Surprising," *BeliefNet*, January 2024, https://www.beliefnet.com/columnists/christnewstoday/2024/01/we-asked-7454-christians-how-often-they-prayand-the-results-were-surprising.html.
2. "Daily Time Spent on Social Media in the United States in 2023, by Age Group," *Statista*, https://www.statista.com/statistics/1484565/time-spent-social-media-us-by-age.
3. Orr, *The History of Revival and Spiritual Awakenings*, "The Awakening of 1792 Onward."
4. Ibid.
5. Clark, *A Table in the Frontier*, 39.
6. Ibid., 76.
7. Orr, *The History of Revival and Spiritual Awakenings*, "The Awakening of 1792 Onward."
8. Ibid.

CHAPTER 5:

1. *The Korea Pentecost* (Board of Foreign Missions of the Presbyterian Church), 45.
2. Orr, *The History of Revival and Spiritual Awakenings*, "The Awakening of 1858–59 in America."

3. Orr, *The History of Revival and Spiritual Awakenings*, "The Awakening of 1904 in Wales."

CHAPTER 6:

1. "Why Americans Go to Religious Services," *Pew Research Center*, August 1, 2018, https://www.pewresearch.org/religion/2018/08/01/why-americans-go-to-religious-services.
2. "U.S. Religion Census," https://www.usreligioncensus.org.
3. "The State of Church Membership," ChurchTrac, https://www.churchtrac.com/articles/the-state-of-church-membership.
4. "America's Changing Religious Landscape," *Pew Research Center*, May 12, 2015, https://www.pewresearch.org/religion/2015/05/12/americas-changing-religious-landscape.
5. "The State of Church Attendance: Trends and Statistics (2023)," ChurchTrac, https://www.churchtrac.com/articles/the-state-of-church-attendance-trends-and-statistics-2023.
6. McLoughlin, *Revivals, Awakenings, and Reform*, 66.
7. "The Way We Weren't: Religion in Colonial America," *The Washington Post*, November 25, 1995.
8. Edward O'Donnell, *Turning Points in American History*, Course Guidebook, 58.
9. Iain H. Murray, *Revival and Revivalism* (Bath: The Bath Press, 1994), 113.
10. J. Edwin Orr, *The Light of the Nations* (Eugene, OR: Wipf & Stock, 2006), 28.
11. Ibid.
12. Ibid., 29.
13. Clark, *A Table in the Frontier*, 91.
14. Orr, *The History of Revival and Spiritual Awakenings*, "The Awakening of 1858–59 in America."
15. Orr, *The History of Revival and Spiritual Awakenings*, "The Awakening of 1904 in Wales."
16. Ibid.
17. Ibid.
18. Ibid.

19. *The Korea Pentecost*, 45.
20. Orr, *The History of Revival and Spiritual Awakenings*, "The Awakening of 1858–59 in America."

CHAPTER 7:

1. Edward O'Donnell, *Turning Points in American History*, Lecture 18, College of the Holy Cross.
2. Robert Davidson, *Presbyterian Church in Kentucky*, 136.
3. Ernest Thompson, *Presbyterians in the South*, vol. 1 (Richmond: John Knox Press, 1963), 138–39.
4. Orr, *The History of Revival and Spiritual Awakenings*, "The Awakening of 1904 in Wales."
5. Ibid.
6. Ibid.

CHAPTER 8:

1. McLoughlin, *Revivals, Awakenings, and Reform*, 10.
2. Ibid., 51.
3. Ibid., 66.
4. Ibid., 67.
5. "Was America Founded as a Christian Nation?" *Associated Press*, https://apnews.com/article/american-founders-christian-nation-conservative-beliefs-4ea388e8d80c54016a6a4460cbef9b82.
6. Thomas Kidd, *Benjamin Franklin: The Religious Life of a Founding Father* (New Haven: Yale University Press, 2017), 1.
7. Ibid., 36.
8. Arthur B. Strickland, *The Great American Revival* (Cincinnati: Standard Press, 1934), 36.
9. Orr, *The History of Revival and Spiritual Awakenings*, "The Awakening of 1792 Onward."
10. Clark, *A Table in the Frontier*, 29.
11. Ibid., 37.

12. Thompson, *Presbyterians in the South*, 138–39.
13. *From Jerusalem to Irian Jaya*, 109.
14. Orr, *The Light of the Nations*, 17.
15. Ibid., 45.
16. Orr, *The History of Revival and Spiritual Awakenings*, "The Awakening of 1858–59 in America."
17. Ibid.
18. *From Jerusalem to Irian Jaya*, 109.
19. Orr, *The Light of the Nations*, 211.
20. Thompson, *Life of A. B. Simpson*, 227.
21. Orr, *The History of Revival and Spiritual Awakenings*, "The Awakening of 1858–59 in America."
22. "Revival and Collapse: Billy Sunday's Fiery Campaign in Burlington, Iowa (1905)," *Evangelist Billy Sunday*, https://evangelistbillysunday.com/2025/04/06/revival-and-collapse-billy-sundays-fiery-campaign-in-burlington-iowa-1905.

For more info, visit

REALREVIVAL.COM